Quick Start Guide to Dart Programming

Create High-Performance Applications for the Web and Mobile

Sanjib Sinha

Apress®

Quick Start Guide to Dart Programming

Sanjib Sinha
Howrah, West Bengal, India

ISBN-13 (pbk): 978-1-4842-5561-2   ISBN-13 (electronic): 978-1-4842-5562-9
https://doi.org/10.1007/978-1-4842-5562-9

Managing Director, Apress Media LLC: Welmoed Spahr
Acquisitions Editor: Nikhil Karkal
Development Editor: Matthew Moodie
Coordinating Editor: Divya Modi

Cover designed by eStudioCalamar

Cover image designed by Pixabay

Distributed to the book trade worldwide by Springer Science+Business Media New York, 233 Spring Street, 6th Floor, New York, NY 10013. Phone 1-800-SPRINGER, fax (201) 348-4505, e-mail orders-ny@springer-sbm.com, or visit www.springeronline.com. Apress Media, LLC is a California LLC and the sole member (owner) is Springer Science + Business Media Finance Inc (SSBM Finance Inc). SSBM Finance Inc is a **Delaware** corporation.

For information on translations, please e-mail rights@apress.com, or visit www.apress.com/rights-permissions.

Apress titles may be purchased in bulk for academic, corporate, or promotional use. eBook versions and licenses are also available for most titles. For more information, reference our Print and eBook Bulk Sales web page at www.apress.com/bulk-sales.

Any source code or other supplementary material referenced by the author in this book is available to readers on GitHub via the book's product page, located at www.apress.com/978-1-4842-5561-2. For more detailed information, please visit www.apress.com/source-code.

Printed on acid-free paper

*To Arun Sengupta and Dipali Sengupta,
my elder brother and sister-in-law, the people closest to my
heart. Although we are locationally challenged, living in
different places, we are separated only by space. Wherever
we live, we will always be together in our minds.*

Table of Contents

About the Author ix

About the Technical Reviewer xi

Acknowledgments xiii

Introduction xv

Chapter 1: Getting Started with Dart 1

The Core Features of Dart 2

Using an IDE for Dart... 4

Installing IntelliJ IDEA Community Edition.. 7

Installing Android Studio... 9

Writing Some Dart Code 11

Variables, Operators, Conditionals, and Control Flow 14

Variables Store References 14

Built-in Types in Dart 17

Suppose You Don't Like Variables... 18

Playing with Number and Double 19

Understanding Strings 22

To Be True or to Be False 26

Introduction to Collections: Arrays Are Lists in Dart 27

Get, Set, Go... 29

Operators Are Useful... 33

Relational Operators 35

Type Test Operators 38

Assignment Operators 39

Summary 41

Chapter 2: Flow Control and Looping 43

if-else 43

Conditional Expressions 49

Looking at Looping 50

for Loop 50

while and do-while 53

Patterns in Looping 56

Summary 65

Chapter 3: Functions and Objects 67

Functions 67

Objects 73

Digging Deep into Object-Oriented Programming 77

Examining Constructors 81

How to Implement Classes 84

Lexical Scope in Functions 87

A Few Words About Getter and Setter 89

Different Types of Parameters 90

More About Constructors 93

Chapter 4: Inheritance and Mixins in Dart 97

A First Look at Inheritance 98

Multilevel Inheritance 104

Mixins: Adding More Features to a Class 108

Chapter 5: Entity Relationships: Abstract Classes, Interfaces, and Exception Handling...**113**

Identifying Relationships Between Entities..114

Using Abstract Classes...117

Advantages of Interfaces 121

Static Variables and Methods..130

Exception Handling 132

Chapter 6: Anonymous Functions...**141**

A First Look at Lambdas 142

Exploring Higher-Order Functions...145

A Closure Is a Special Function...146

Bringing It All Together...149

Chapter 7: Data Structures and Collections......................................**153**

Lists: An Ordered Collection 155

Set: An Unordered Collections of Unique Items...162

Maps: The Key-Value Pair 166

Using Collections Together..171

Queue Is Open-Ended 176

Chapter 8: Multithreaded Programming Using Future and Callable Classes..**179**

Callable Classes..179

Future, Async, Await, and Asynchronous Programming 182

More on the Future API 197

TABLE OF CONTENTS

Chapter 9: Dart Packages and Libraries 201

Importing Packages 203

Using Built-in Dart Libraries.. 206

Writing a Server Using Dart 206

    Showing Some Simple Text 207

    Showing an HTML Page.. 211

What's Next... 214

Index..215

About the Author

 **Sanjib Sinha** is an author and tech writer. Being a certified .NET Windows and web developer, he specializes in Python security programming and Linux and in many programming languages such as C#, PHP, Python, Dart, Java, and JavaScript. Sanjib won Microsoft's Community Contributor Award in 2011, and he has written the following books for Apress: *Beginning Ethical Hacking with Python*, *Beginning Ethical Hacking with Kali Linux*, *Beginning Laravel 5.8* (first and second editions), and *Bug Bounty Hunting for Web Security*.

About the Technical Reviewer

 **Abir Ranjan Atarthy** is an Offensive Security Certified Professional (OSCP), Certified Ethical Hacker (CEH), and Certified Hacking Forensic Investigator (CHFI).

He has deep expertise in the domain of cybersecurity and different programming languages with more than 10 years of hands-on experience in the areas of network security, vulnerability analysis, penetration testing, web security, security analytics, malware protection, cryptography, data protection, and digital forensics.

He has coded many scripts in Python, Ruby, etc., and has mentored numerous students to create tools/applications in different areas of cybersecurity.

Abir has authored several technical articles that have been published in IT security journals and is frequently invited to speak at cybersecurity conferences and forums. He has been quoted by leading newspapers and TV channels on several occasions as a subject-matter expert.

In addition, he has conducted several workshops and training/certification programs on cybersecurity, Python, secure coding framework, etc., for large corporations, different universities, and engineering colleges.

He has an M.Sc. in computer applications and has finished short-term programs in object-oriented programming in Java and C++, data structure, and aspects of software engineering at the Indian Institute of Technology – Kharagpur.

Currently he is with TCG Digital Solutions Pvt. Ltd.

Acknowledgments

I wish to record my gratitude to my wife, Kaberi, for her unwavering support and encouragement in the preparation of this book.

I am extremely grateful to lead development editor Matthew Moodie for his numerous valuable suggestions, as well as editor Nikhil Karkal, coordinating editor Divya Modi, and the whole Apress team for their consistent support and help.

I am also thankful to the technical reviewer, Abir Atarthi, for his valuable observations in a short period of time, and to the Google developers who created this beautiful language called Dart, which is simple to learn and elegant.

In the preparation of this book, I consulted numerous open source documentation and textbooks on a variety of subjects related to Dart, especially the Dart documentation and libraries, so I thank the countless authors and writers of them.

Introduction

Dart is a great fit for both mobile apps and web apps. Dart is free and open source, and the repository is available at `https://github.com/dart-lang`. You can also get a feel of the language at the official web site: `https://www.dartlang.org/`.

In this book, you will come to understand why learning the Dart language is important to build mission-critical mobile apps on iOS and Android.

Developers around the world use Dart to create high-quality apps for iOS and Android and for the Web. It is feature rich so that client-side development is also possible. As you progress throughout the book, you will see how correct this statement is.

If you want to learn how to build native iOS and Android mobile apps and web apps using Dart, then this book serves as a good introduction because it is designed to give you a complete picture of how Dart works.

CHAPTER 1

Getting Started with Dart

So, why the Dart language? Well, Dart is a great fit for both mobile apps and web apps. Dart is free and open source, and the repository is available at `https://github.com/dart-lang`. You can also get a feel of the language at the official web site: `https://www.dartlang.org/`. The advantage of Dart is, since it is a client optimized programming language for apps on multiple platforms, you can use it for as many purposes as Desktop, Mobile, backend, and web applications. Another advantage is it can be transcompiled into JavaScript, if you want.

In this introductory chapter, let's try to understand why learning the Dart language is important for building mission-critical mobile apps on iOS and Android. If you already have a working knowledge in Object Oriented Language like Java or Python, it will be much easier for you to understand the core concepts because using C-style syntax, Dart is a class-defined, garbage collected language.

Developers around the world use Dart to create high-quality apps for iOS and Android and the Web. It is feature rich so that client-side development is also possible. As we progress throughout the book, you will see how correct this statement is.

If you want to learn how to build native iOS and Android mobile apps and web apps using Dart, then this book serves as a good introduction because it is designed to give you a complete picture of how Dart works.

© Sanjib Sinha 2020
S. Sinha, *Quick Start Guide to Dart Programming*,
https://doi.org/10.1007/978-1-4842-5562-9_1

Though building a full mobile app is beyond the scope of this book, you will build a simple web app in Chapter 9.

The Core Features of Dart

Figure 1-1 shows the core features of the Dart programming language.

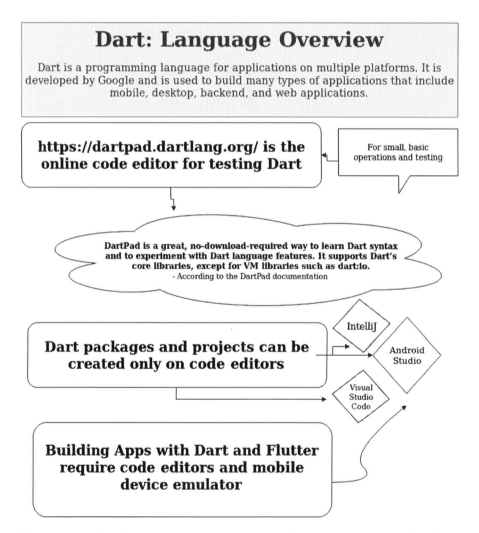

Figure 1-1. *The Dart language overview and how we can use code editors*

For small operations, you can use the online code editor at `https://dartpad.dartlang.org`. However, for building packages and creating projects, you need a code editor like Android Studio or IntelliJ IDEA Community Edition. Visual Studio Code also has Dart language testing support. But using Android Studio or IntelliJ IDEA Community Edition is recommended. They make it easy to install the required plugins; furthermore, if you want to build mobile applications using Dart and Flutter, these tools are more useful.

Note   These code editors are known as *integrated development environments* (IDEs). They have lots of features that make writing code easy and efficient. In other words, they are designed to make your coding life easier.

First, Dart is extremely productive. If you already know an object-oriented programming language such as C++, C#, or Java, it will not take you more than a few days to learn the Dart language. If you are an absolute beginner, then it is good that you are starting to learn Dart as your first programming language because it has a clear and concise syntax. It also has rich and powerful core libraries and supports thousands of packages. As an absolute beginner, you don't have to worry about the libraries right now. You will learn to use them later in the book when the time comes.

Syntax-wise, Dart has similarities with C, C#, Python, Java, and JavaScript (Figure 1-2).

Dart Language Features

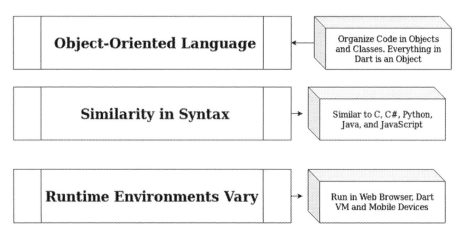

Figure 1-2. *Dart language features at a glance*

Dart is fast and furious, and the performance is high across mobile devices and the Web. In addition, its portability rate is extremely good. It compiles to ARM and x86 code so that Dart mobile apps can run on iOS and Android and beyond.

Beginners should note that there is a difference between ARM and X86 processors; the ARM processors follow a Reduced Instruction Set Computer (RISC) architecture, while x86 processors are Complex Instruction Set Architecture (CISC). Because of these features, x86 processors are considered to be faster than ARM processors.

In addition, for web apps, Dart has a close relationship with Flutter, which is implemented by using Dart code.

Using an IDE for Dart

You can use any good IDE; however, my choice is either IntelliJ IDEA Community Edition or Android Studio. Both are free and can be easily downloaded on Windows, Linux, and Mac.

For the code in this book, you will find IntelliJ IDEA Community Edition the easiest to use. It is designed for general development, whereas Android Studio is designed for mobile development. This means it's easy to start a simple Dart app in IntelliJ but not in Android Studio. In fact, Android Studio does not even have that option. It will allow you to create only a Flutter mobile app. If your goal is mobile development, I recommend you use IntelliJ to learn Dart from this book and then switch to Android Studio for your first Flutter app.

Tip   One work-around to this approach is to create a Dart app in IntelliJ IDEA Community Edition and then open it in Android Studio (with the Dart plugin installed). Android Studio will run the app no problem; it's creating one in the first place that is difficult. You will see I have taken this approach in the book.

There are two options for both IDEs, as Android Studio is basically a customized version of IntelliJ.

- Installing the IDE to test your code with the Dart SDK on your local system.

- Installing Flutter and the Dart plugin in any IDE. In this case, you don't need the Dart SDK on your operating system.

Installing either IDE in Windows is relatively easy. Download the .exe file from the official web site and double-click to launch it. This is the recommended way. You can also download the ZIP file and unpack it to the program files. You will find the bin folder where you can launch the respective .exe files. However, downloading the .exe file from the official web site and launching it online is recommended.

Installing an IDE on a Mac is not a complicated process. You need to launch the DMG file and then drag and drop the app into the Applications folder. After that, the launching process is easy; the setup wizard will guide you through the rest.

I recommend you use Linux as the main operating system; Android as a framework will always execute better on top of the Linux kernel, and it's likely you'll want to use Dart for Android development. Installing the Dart SDK in Linux is also easy.

Why do you need the Dart SDK? Well, it has the libraries and command-line tools that you need to develop all kinds of Dart applications—web, command-line, or server apps. To develop only mobile apps, you don't need the Dart SDK. The Flutter plugins in the IDE will work.

To install Dart on Linux, first open your terminal, and then you can issue the following commands:

```
//code 1.1
sudo apt-get update

sudo apt-get install apt-transport-https

 sudo sh -c 'curl https://dl-ssl.google.com/linux/linux_
 signing_key.pub | apt-key add -'

 sudo sh -c 'curl https://storage.googleapis.com/download.
 dartlang.org/linux/debian/dart_stable.list > /etc/apt/sources.
 list.d/dart_stable.list'
```

After that, install the stable release of the Dart SDK.

```
//code 1.2
sudo apt-get update

 sudo apt-get install dart
```

After that you can check your Dart version.

```
//code 1.3
$ dart --version
Dart VM version: 2.4.0 (Unknown timestamp) on "linux_x64"
```

The Dart SDK includes a lib directory for the Dart libraries that you will use in the IDE. In addition, the Dart SDK has a bin directory that has the command-line tools. It helps run the console inside your IDE, and you can also have the terminal output, if you want. For that, you can go to the project's bin folder and run the main.dart file.

Installing IntelliJ IDEA Community Edition

Installing IntelliJ IDEA Community Edition is easy. You can install it from the Ubuntu Software Center. Open the Software Center and type **IntelliJ Community Edition**. It will show up. Click the Install button (Figure 1-3).

Figure 1-3. *Launching IntelliJ*

You can also install IntelliJ IDEA Community Edition through the command line on the terminal.

```
//code 1.4
sudo snap install intellij-idea-community –classic
```

The applications in the Ubuntu Software Center are snap packages; therefore, if you already have snap packages installed in your machine, you can install it through the terminal. After the primary installation is done, don't forget to install the Dart plugins, either from the Configure option at startup or from File ➤ Settings ➤ Plugins within the IDE (Figure 1-4).

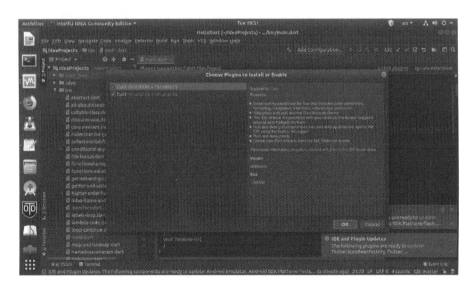

Figure 1-4. *Installing or enabling the Dart plugins*

Finally, IntelliJ IDEA Community Edition is ready for action. Figure 1-5 shows some projects from the book. You can keep your Dart files in the bin folder and run the program by pressing Shift+F10 or selecting Run ➤ Run from the menu bar. Most of the example code will print to the console at the bottom of the IDE.

Figure 1-5. *IntelliJ IDEA Community Edition and the console*

Installing Android Studio

Installing Android Studio on Linux is quite simple and user friendly, though not as straightforward as installing IntelliJ IDEA Community Edition.

You don't have to issue any command-line instructions. Download the ZIP file and unpack it to either /usr/local/ or /opt/ for shared users. Now, navigate to the /android-studio/bin/ directory and execute the studio.sh file with the help of this command:

```
//code 1.5
./studio.sh
```

If it asks you to install the required libraries for 64-bit Linux machines, install them. If you are a first-time user of Android Studio, you can import the previous Android Studio settings or you can skip this by clicking the OK button.

The Android Studio wizard will guide you to set it up; remember, this setup includes downloading Android SDK components that are required for development; in the Configure option when you start the IDE, you can install the Flutter and Dart plugins (or select File ➤ Settings ➤ Plugins when the IDE is open).

Figure 1-6 displays Android Studio.

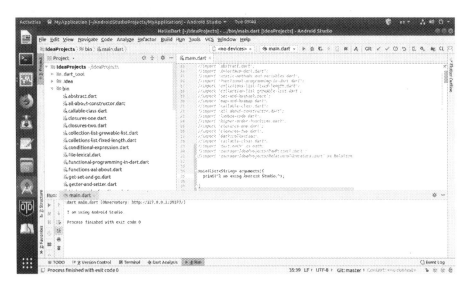

Figure 1-6. *The Android Studio IDE and the Dart files in the bin folder*

To get maximum use of Android Studio on a 64-bit Linux machine, say Ubuntu, you need to install some 32-bit libraries with the following command-line instructions. You can access these libraries through your project's lib folder. The bin folder consists of command-line tools, as I have mentioned earlier.

```
//code 1.6
sudo apt-get install libc6:i386 libncurses5:i386
libstdc++6:i386 lib32z1 libbz2-1.0:i386
```

The command will ask you for the root password. For the 64-bit Fedora, the command is different.

```
//code 1.7
sudo yum install zlib.i686 ncurses-libs.i686 bzip2-libs.i686
```

Now, you are ready to work in Android Studio.

Writing Some Dart Code

Let's look at our first Dart code. Put the following code into your main.dart file in your IDE. main() is the entry point, not only for Dart; if you build mobile apps using Flutter, you will find that in Flutter, this is the entry point as well.

```
//code 1.8
main() {
  print("Hello World!");
}
//output
Hello World!
```

In Android Studio or IntelliJ, you can press Shift+F10 to run the code.

Let's write some more console-based code to get a feel for Dart. At the same time, you will see the most basic syntax and how the commands work together.

```
//code 1.9
main() {
  print("Hello World!");
  //calling a function
  doSomething();
}
```

```
//define a function
doSomething(){
  print("Do something!")
  //calling a function inside another function
     lifeIsShort();
}
//defining another function
lifeIsShort(){
  print("Life is too short to do so many things.");
}
```

We have started our code with the top-level function main(); it is required and special in nature because this is how the application executes. So, inside the main() function, we have called a function doSomething(), which in turn calls the lifeIsShort() function.

Each function gives a display output with print(); this is a handy way to display any output. We have covered many things in our first program. Now run the code (Shift+F10).

You'll see there is a mistake in our code. It is an intended mistake so that you understand how debugging takes place in Dart.

Take a look at the output:

```
//output of code 1.9
bin/main.dart:12:24: Error: Expected ';' after this.
  print("Do something!")
```

We have forgotten to place a semicolon after displaying the output.

```
//code 1.10
//define a function
doSomething(){
  print("Do something!");
```

```
//calling a function inside another function
lifeIsShort();
}
```

Let's correct it and run the program again.

```
//output of code 1.10
Hello World!
Do something!
Life is too short to do so many things.
```

Now it is OK. You have learned many things with this first code; most important is that we can learn from our mistakes.

You should always be careful about syntax errors. Missing a semicolon or a dollar sign before a variable can be a big game-changer.

You have seen how we comment on our code with // characters, as shown here:

```
//calling a function inside another function
lifeIsShort();
```

Anything on that line is ignored when the program runs. Try to contribute as much comments as possible to make clear your viewpoint so that when another person reads your code, they will understand it and visualize it as you have visualized your code while writing it. The person who reads your code in six months may well be you, so be kind to your future self.

If you are a complete beginner, you may be at a loss to understand these explanations. You may feel puzzled about words such as *function, comment, output,* etc. Therefore, the next few sections are dedicated to beginners.

Variables, Operators, Conditionals, and Control Flow

In this section, we will discuss some initial key concepts of Dart that are absolutely necessary for beginners. First, like Python, Dart is an object-oriented programming language. Everything is an object here.

Consider a whole number like 2. In nature, it is an integer. In Dart, all integers are objects. Even functions and null are objects. I know, the term *object* may fill a beginner with bewilderment. We will discuss object-oriented programming at the right time. Before that, you will learn what variables, constants, and functions are.

Note   Briefly, null means that a data value does not exist. Since Dart considers every value type as an object, a null class has also been created to use that instance where no value is provided.

Variables Store References

Variables store references to objects. In other words, you may say, a variable is a spot in the memory or a container that contains some references to some values. As indicated by the name *variable*, the reference can change.

Like other programming languages, Dart has several types, such as integers, strings, Booleans, etc. Although Dart is strongly typed language, it also allows you to use duck typing, meaning that Dart can use a type as long as that type is suitable for that use ("If it walks like a duck and quacks like a duck, it is a duck").

Data types are types of data that we can represent in a programming language, such as an integer is a nonfractional numerical value like 1, 2, and so on. Later when needed, we can also manipulate these values in our program. For example, in a calculator we do lots of numerical operations such as additions, subtractions, etc. The default value of most data types is null. So, we need to mention what data type we are going to use.

We use variables to reference those types that are actually stored in memory. Consider the following:

```
int a = 1;
```

This means we first store the type of integer value 1 in our memory, and then we assign that value to the variable a. The equal sign (=) is the assignment operator in Dart, so it assigns values to variables. Later, we call a to grab 1 for any kind of mathematical operations.

In normal circumstances, in Dart, we mention what type we are going to use. If we use integers and strings, we write it like this:

```
//code 1.11
int myAge = 12;
String myName = "John Smith";
```

In the previous examples, we have explicitly declared the type that should be used. In the next example, we do the same thing, but implicitly.

Therefore, you can also write the same code in this way:

```
//code 1.12
var myAge = 12;
var myName = "John Smith";
```

Now, the question is, with a change of reference, does the type also change?

Please read on.

In the previous code snippets, variable myAge stores the value 12 and references it as an integer object. The same way, the myName variable stores the value John Smith and references it as a String object. The type of the myName variable is inferred to be string-specific, but you can change it. If you don't want a specific or restricted type, specify Object or dynamic type.

```
dynamic myName = "John Smith";
```

If you don't initialize a variable, the default value is set to be null. Let's consider the following code:

```
int myNumber;
```

Although it is an integer, it is not initialized. Therefore, the default value is Null. Let's run the code and take a look at the output.

```
//code 1.13
main() {
  print("Hello World!");
  int myNumber;
  print(myNumber);
}
```

The output is as expected:

```
Hello World!
null
```

Let's talk about the built-in types in Dart. So far you have seen some of the types, such as number and string. You have not seen the others.

Built-in Types in Dart

The Dart language has special support for the following types, and you can always follow the strongly typed or duck typed pattern to initialize them:

- Numbers

- Strings

- Booleans

- Lists (also known as arrays)

- Sets

- Maps

- Runes (for expressing Unicode characters in a string)

- Symbols

You can initialize an object of any of these special types using a literal. For example, Hello John Smith is a string literal, and false is a Boolean literal.

Consider this code:

```
//code 1.14
main() {
  String saySomething = "Hello John Smith";
  var isFalse = true;
  if(saySomething == null){
    print("It is ${isFalse}");
  }else print("It is not ${isFalse}");
}
```

Since the string variable is not null, the output should be as follows:

```
It is not true
```

Note   We use ${} to include the value of an expression in a string. In this case, it is the value of a variable converted to a string. Including the value of an expression in this way is called *string interpolation*. I'll cover that later in the chapter.

You will encounter the first four built-in types most often. You will learn how to use other built-in types as the situation demands.

Suppose You Don't Like Variables

Well, in some cases, you need the value to be constant. There are two techniques that you can follow when you don't intend to change the value of a variable.

- You can use const instead of var or a String, int, or bool type declaration.

- You can also use final; but remember, the final variable can be set only once.

So, there is a difference between these two keywords: const and final. We will come back to this topic when we discuss object-oriented programming. Note that an instance variable can be final but not const.

Consider this code:

```
//code 1.15
main() {
  const firstName = "Sanjib";
  final lastName = "Sinha";
  String firstName = "John";
  String lastName = "Sinha";
}
```

Look at the output full of errors:

```
//output
bin/main.dart:8:10: Error: 'firstName' is already declared in
this scope.
  String firstName = "John";
         ^^^^^^^^^
bin/main.dart:5:9: Context: Previous declaration of 'firstName'.
  const firstName = "Sanjib";
        ^^^^^^^^^
bin/main.dart:9:10: Error: 'lastName' is already declared in
this scope.
  String lastName = "Sinha";
         ^^^^^^^^
bin/main.dart:6:9: Context: Previous declaration of 'lastName'.
  final lastName = "Sinha";
```

When you want a variable to be a compile-time constant, use const; use final for an instance variable that you will never change.

As a quick review, we will first check the numbers. Then one after another, you will learn about string, Booleans, and other types.

Dart numbers are of two types: integers and decimals. You write them as int and double. Integers are numbers without decimal points. Examples are 1, 2, 22, etc. Doubles do have a decimal point like this: 1.5, 3.723, etc.

Playing with Number and Double

Both int and double types are subtypes of num. The num type includes basic operators such as +, -, /, and *; and they represent plus, minus, division, and multiplication, respectively. You can call them arithmetic operators. There is also modulo, that is, remainder, and the sign is %.

Let's see some interesting examples:

```dart
//code 1.16
main() {
  var one = int.parse('1');
  print(one);
  if(one.isOdd){
    print("It is an odd number.");
  } else print("It is an even number.");
}
```

We have converted a string into an integer, or number.

```
//output
1
It is an odd number.
```

We can also turn a string into a double number. Let's change the previous code a little bit.

```dart
//code 1.17
main() {
  var one = int.parse('1');
  var doubleToString = double.parse('23.564');
  print(one);
  print(doubleToString);
  if(one.isOdd && doubleToString.isFinite){
    print("The first number is an odd number and the second one
    is a double ${doubleToString} and a finite number.");
  } else print("It is an even number and the second one is not
  a double ${doubleToString} and a non-finite number.");
}
```

The output is quite expected. Both statements are true, so the relational operation gives this output:

```
//output
1
23.564
A first number is an odd number and the second one is a double
23.564 and a finite number.
```

We can do the reverse too. We are going to turn an integer to string here:

```
//code 1.18
main() {
  int myNUmber = 542;
  double myDouble = 3.42;
  String numberToString = myNUmber.toString();
  String doubleToString = myDouble.toString();
  if ((numberToString == '542' && myNUmber.isEven) &&
  (doubleToString == '3.42' && myDouble.isFinite)){
    print("Both have been converted from an even number
    ${myNUmber} and a finite double ${myDouble} to string. ");
  } else print("Number and double have not been converted to
  string.");
}
//output
```

Both have been converted from the even number 542 and the finite double 3.42 to a string.

As we progress, we will find that Dart is an extremely flexible language, and the syntax is simple to remember with lots of help from the core libraries.

Understanding Strings

A Dart string is a sequence of UTF-16 code units. For absolute beginners, I'll briefly describe UTF-8, UTF-16, and UTF-32. They all store Unicode but use different bytes. Let's first try to understand the advantages of using UTF-16 code over the other two. Let's learn about UTF-8.

In places where ASCII characters represent the majority of text, UTF-8 has an advantage. ASCII is meant for English only because it started in the United States. Later it spread all over the world, and other countries were eager to get strings to work on their languages. Like ASCII, UTF-8 encodes all characters into 8 bits.

Where ASCII is not predominant (in cultures where English is not predominant), UTF-16 has an advantage.

Using 2 bytes (16 bits) enables us to encode 65,536 distinct values. If you are serious about understanding encodings and character sets, please visit this link:

```
http://kunststube.net/encoding/
```

UTF-16 remains at just 2 bytes for most characters. However, UTF-32 tries to cover all possible characters in 4 bytes, which means that processors have extra load, making UTF-32 pretty bloated. Simply put, it is all about supporting as many languages as possible.

Unicode support makes Dart more powerful, and you can create your mobile and web applications in any language. Let's see one example where I have tried some Bengali script.

```
//code 1.19
main(List<String> arguments) {
  String bengaliString = "বাংলা লেখো";
  String englishString = "This is some English text.";
  print("Here is some Bengali script - ${bengaliString} and
  some English script ${englishString}");
}
```

```
Here is some Bengali script - বাংলা লেখা and some English script
This is some English text.
```

While handling strings, you should remember a few things. You can use both single quotes (") and double quotes ("").

```
//code 1.20
main(List<String> arguments) {
  String stringWithSingleQuote = 'I\'m a single quote';
  String stringWithDoubleQuote = "I'm a double quote.";
  print("Using delimiter in single quote -
  ${stringWithSingleQuote} and using delimiter in double
  quote - ${stringWithDoubleQuote}");
}
```

You can use the delimiter in both cases, but the double quote is more helpful in such cases. Look at the output:

```
//output of code 1.21
Using delimiter in the single quote - I'm a single quote and
using delimiter in the double quote - I'm a double quote
```

We have put the value of the expression inside a string by using our variable in this way: ${stringWithSingleQuote}. As noted earlier in the chapter, this is called *string interpolation.*

If you simply want to express the value of a variable, you do not have to use {}. You can use the variable in this way:

```
print("$stringWithSingleQuote");
print(stringWithSingleQuote);
```

String concatenation and even making it multiline is quite easy in Dart. Consider this code:

```
//code 1.22
main(List<String> arguments) {
  String stringInterpolation = 'string ' + 'concatenation';
  print(stringInterpolation);
  String multiLIneString = """
     This is
     a multi line
     string.
  """;
  print(multiLIneString);
}
```

You use the + operator for concatenation, meaning you join two strings together. Looking at the output here, we have used a triple quote with either single or double quotation marks:

```
//output
string concatenation
     This is
     a multi line
     string.
```

If you want to store some constant value inside a constant string, the value cannot be variables. Consider this code:

```
//code 1.23
main(List<String> arguments) {
  const aConstantInteger = 12;
  const aConstantBoolean = true;
  const aConstantString = "I am a constant string.";
```

```
  const aValidConstantString = "this is a constant integer:
  ${aConstantInteger}, a constant boolean: ${aConstantBoolean},
  a constant string: ${aConstantString}";
  print("This is a valid constant string and the output is:
  $aValidConstantString");
}
```

We have created a valid constant string by storing a constant value inside them. The output is perfectly OK.

```
//output
This is a valid constant string and the output is: this is a
constant integer: 12, a constant boolean: true, a constant
string: I am a constant string.
```

This will not work if you want to hold variable data inside a constant string. We have changed the previous code listing to this:

```
//code 1.24
main(List<String> arguments) {
  var aConstantInteger = 12;
  var aConstantBoolean = true;
  var aConstantString = "I am a constant string.";
  const aValidConstantString = "this is a constant integer:
  ${aConstantInteger}, a constant boolean: ${aConstantBoolean},
  a constant string: ${aConstantString}";
  print("This is a valid constant string and the output is:
  $aValidConstantString");
}
```

Here is the output, which is full of errors:

```
//output
```

```
bin/main.dart:9:63: Error: Not a constant expression.
  const aValidConstantString = "this is a constant integer:
  ${aConstantInteger}, a constant boolean: ${aConstantBoolean},
  a constant string: ${aConstantString}";
                                                ^^^^^^^^^^^^^^^^
bin/main.dart:9:104: Error: Not a constant expression.
  const aValidConstantString = "this is a constant integer:
  ${aConstantInteger}, a constant boolean: ${aConstantBoolean},
  a constant string: ${aConstantString}";
                                                ^^^^^^^^^^^^^^^^
bin/main.dart:9:144: Error: Not a constant expression.
  const aValidConstantString = "this is a constant integer:
  ${aConstantInteger}, a constant boolean: ${aConstantBoolean},
  a constant string: ${aConstantString}";
```

It did not work. As we progress, you will learn more about strings. Understanding them is important in the context of making mobile and web applications.

In the next section, you will learn about Booleans, which also play a vital role in building algorithms.

To Be True or to Be False

You have already seen that Dart has a type called bool. The Boolean literals true and false have the type bool. They are compile-time constants.

This is an extremely important concept in computer science because you can use control structures to alter the flow of your program that depends on whether a statement is true or false. We will cover this in Chapter 2.

Introduction to Collections: Arrays Are Lists in Dart

An *array*, or an ordered group of objects, is the most common collection in every programming language. In Dart, arrays are List objects. We will call them *lists* in our future discussions.

Dart is designed to compile to JavaScript to run across the modern Web; therefore, if you have a working knowledge of JavaScript, you will find some similarities in this type of collection.

Here is some sample code to consider so you can understand why this concept is important:

```
//code 1.25
main(List<String> arguments) {
  List fruitCollection = ['Mango', 'Apple', 'Jack fruit'];
  print(fruitCollection[0]);
}
```

Consider another piece of code:

```
//code 2.15
main(List<String> arguments) {
  List fruitCollection = ['Mango', 'Apple', 'Jack fruit'];
  var myIntegers = [1, 2, 3];
  print(myIntegers[2]);
  print(fruitCollection[0]);
}
```

What is the difference between these two code snippets? In code 2.14, we have explicitly mentioned that we are going to declare a collection of fruits. And we can pick any item from that collection using the key. In an array, the key is not mentioned in the definition; it is automatically inferred that the key starts from 0. Therefore, the output of code 2.14 is Mango. In the second instance, we do not have any explicit declaration about the type of the myIntegers list. We have written this:

```
var myIntegers = [1, 2, 3];
```

However, Dart infers that the list has type List<int>. Let's see the output of code 2.15:

```
//output
3
Mango
```

If we try to inject noninteger objects to the myInteger list, what happens?

```
//code 2.17
main(List<String> arguments) {
  List fruitCollection = ['Mango', 'Apple', 'Jack fruit'];
  var myIntegers = [1, 2, 3, 'non-integer object'];
  print(myIntegers[3]);
  print(fruitCollection[0]);
}
```

This did not raise any error. See the output, shown here:

```
//output of code 2.17
non-integer object
Mango
```

However, remember that Dart lists use zero-based indexing like all the other collections you may have seen in other programming languages. Just think of a list as a key-value pair, where 0 is the index of the first value or element. As we progress, we will discuss lists because there are other useful methods that we will use when we build our first mobile application. Dart lists have many handy methods.

Get, Set, Go

In Dart, a Set is an unordered collection of unique items. There are small differences in syntax between List and Set.

Let's look at an example first to know more about the differences.

```
//code 1.26
main(List<String> arguments) {
  var fruitCollection = {'Mango', 'Apple', 'Jack fruit'};
  print(fruitCollection.lookup('Apple'));
}
//output
Apple
```

We can search a set using the lookup() method. If we search for something else, it returns null.

```
//code 1.27
main(List<String> arguments) {
  var fruitCollection = {'Mango', 'Apple', 'Jack fruit'};
  print(fruitCollection.lookup('Something Else'));
}
//output
null
```

When we write the following, it does not create a Set, but a Map:

```
var myInteger = {};
```

The syntax for map literals is similar to that for set literals. Why is this? Because map literals came first. The literal {} is a default to the Map type. We can prove this by using this simple test:

```
//code 1.28
main(List<String> arguments) {
  var myInteger = {};
```

```
  if(myInteger.isEmpty){
    print("It is a map that has no key, value pair.");
  } else print("It is a set that has no key, value pair.");
}
```

Look at the output:

```
//output of code 2.20
```

This is a map that has no key-value pair. It means the map is empty. If it were a set, we would have gotten the output in that direction. We will see lots of examples of sets in the future, while we build our mobile application. For now, just remember that, in general, a map is an object that associates keys with values. The set has also keys, but they are implicit. In cases of sets, we call them *indexes*.

Let's see one example of the Map type by mapping literals. While writing keys and values, it is important to note that each key occurs only once, but you can use the same value many times.

```
//code 1.29
main(List<String> arguments) {
  var myProducts = {
    'first' : 'TV',
    'second' : 'Refrigerator',
    'third' : 'Mobile',
    'fourth' : 'Tablet',
    'fifth' : 'Computer'
  };
  print(myProducts['third']);
}
```

The output is obvious, as shown here:

```
'Mobile'
```

Dart understands that myProducts has the type Map<String, String>(Map<Key, Value>); we could have made the key integers or numbers, instead of a string type.

```
//code 1.30
main(List<String> arguments) {
  var myProducts = {
    1 : 'TV',
    2 : 'Refrigerator',
    3 : 'Mobile',
    4 : 'Tablet',
    5 : 'Computer'
  };
  print(myProducts[3]);
}
```

The output is the same as before: mobile.

Can we add a Set type collection of values inside a Map? Yes, we can. Consider this code:

```
//code 1.31
main(List<String> arguments) {
  Set mySet = {1, 2, 3};
  var myProducts = {
    1 : 'TV',
    2 : 'Refrigerator',
    3 : mySet.lookup(2),
    4 : 'Tablet',
    5 : 'Computer'
  };
  print(myProducts[3]);
}
```

In the previous code, we injected a collection of the Set type, and we also looked up the defining value through the Map key. Here, inside the Map key-value pair, we have added the set element number 2 in this way: 3 : mySet.lookup(2). Later we tell our Android Studio editor to display the value of the Map type myProducts.

The output is quite expected: 2.

You can create the same products list by using the Map constructor. For beginners, the term *constructor* might seem difficult. We will discuss this term in detail in Chapter 7. Consider this code:

```
//code 1.32
main(List<String> arguments) {
  var myProducts = Map();
  myProducts['first'] ='TV';
  myProducts['second'] ='Mobile';
  myProducts['third'] ='Refrigerator';
  if(myProducts.containsValue('Mobile')){
    print("Our products list has ${myProducts['second']}");
  }
}
```

Here is the output:

```
//output
Our products list has Mobile
```

Since we have an instance in code 1.32 of the Map class, a seasoned programmer might have expected new Map() instead of only Map().

As of Dart 2, the new keyword is optional. You will learn about it in detail in Chapter 7.

You will also learn more about collections in Chapter 7, where you will learn more about List, Set, and Map.

Operators Are Useful

Simply put, programming is about processing variables. This processing might be to perform a mathematical calculation or to concatenate two strings, for example. For that purpose we need operators. The simplicity of Dart is the + operator adds two integer operands (variables) and produces a result. At the same time, we may use the + operator to concatenate two strings (as shown in code 1.22).

In Dart, when you use operators, you actually create expressions.

Here are some examples of expressions: a++, a + b, a * b, a/b, a~/b, a%b, and so on.

There are many types of operators in Dart. Even absolute beginners probably have heard of arithmetic operators. Relational operators are extremely useful for the control structures.

We will take a look at them one after another.

The usual arithmetic operators are - add (+), subtract (-), multiply (*), divide (/), and modulo or remainder (%); a special operator, divide, returning an integer looks like this: ~/.

Let's see one example:

```
//code 1.33
main(List<String> arguments) {
  int aNum = 12;
  double aDouble = 2.25;
  var theResult = aNum ~/ aDouble;
  print(theResult);
}
//output
5
```

Note this special operator has displayed an integer, not a double. However, if we had divided it in a plain fashion, it would look like this:

```
//code 1.34
main(List<String> arguments) {
  int aNum = 12;
  double aDouble = 2.25;
  var theResult = aNum / aDouble;
  print(theResult);
}
```

Here is the output:

```
//output of code 2.26
5.333333333333333
```

One key feature of Dart is that it supports both prefix and postfix increment and decrement operators.

Here, a prefix means ++variable or --variable. These either add 1 or subtract 1 from the variable value, respectively. The postfix does the same; only the syntax changes, like this: variable++ or variable--.

Let's see an example:

```
//code 1.35
main(List<String> arguments) {
  int aNum = 12;
  aNum++;
  ++aNum;
  int anotherNum = aNum + 1;
  print(anotherNum);
}
```

The output is as expected: 15. Both prefix and postfix work in the case of -- also.

Relational Operators

Relational operators are also called *equality operators* because == means "equal," and other relational operators usually check for equality in various forms.

Let's consider some code snippets that will show us many types of relational operators in one glance.

```
//code 1.36
main(List<String> arguments) {
  int firstNum = 40;
  int secondNum = 41;
  if (firstNum != secondNum){
    print("$firstNum is not equal to the $secondNum");
  } else print("$firstNum is equal to the $secondNum");
}
//output
40 is not equal to the 41
```

In the previous code, the != operator stands for "not equal." It comes out true if the operands are not equal. So, we're saying "If firstNum does not equal secondNum, execute the code between {}. Otherwise, execute the code after the else."

Let's change this code a little bit:

```
//code 1.37
main(List<String> arguments) {
  int firstNum = 40;
  int secondNum = 40;
  if (firstNum == secondNum){
    print("$firstNum is equal to the $secondNum");
  } else print("$firstNum is not equal to the $secondNum");
}
```

Here we're saying "If firstNum equals secondNum, execute the code between {}. Otherwise, execute the code after the else." Let's add some more logic to our code, as shown here:

```
//code 1.38
main(List<String> arguments) {
  int firstNum = 40;
  int secondNum = 40;
  int thirdNum = 74;
  int fourthNum = 56;
  if (firstNum == secondNum || thirdNum == fourthNum){
    print("If choice between 'true' or 'false', the 'true' gets
    the precedence.");
  } else print("If choice between 'true' or 'false', the
  'false' gets the precedence.");
}
//output
If choice between 'true' or 'false', the 'true' gets the
precedence.
```

This time we're saying "If firstNum equals secondNum OR if thirdNum equals fourthNum, execute the code between {}. Otherwise, execute the code after the else." We use the OR (||) operator to implement this logic. So if one side of the OR operator is true, the whole statement is true.

This is not the case for the AND (&&) relational operator. Look at this code:

```
//code 1.39
main(List<String> arguments) {
  int firstNum = 40;
  int secondNum = 40;
  int thirdNum = 74;
  int fourthNum = 56;
```

```
if (firstNum == secondNum && thirdNum == fourthNum){
  print("If choice between 'true' or 'false', in this case
  the 'true' gets the precedence.");
} else print("If choice between 'true' or 'false', in this
case the 'false' gets the precedence.");
}

//output
If choice between 'true' or 'false', in this case the 'false'
gets the precedence.
```

We have used the && relational operator, and here the expression is false because both sides have to be true in the case of the AND operator. The ! sign has many roles. Consider this code snippet:

```
//code 1.40
main(List<String> arguments) {
  int aNUmber = 35;
  if(!(aNUmber != 150) && aNUmber <= 150){
    print("It's true");
  } else print("It's false.");
}
```

Can you guess what the output would be? The first statement is false because we have negated a true statement by using the ! sign.

```
!(aNUmber != 150)
```

The second statement is true; the value is less than or equal to 150.

```
aNUmber <= 150
```

Since the logical operator is AND (&&) here, the whole expression will be false.

```
!(aNUmber != 150) && aNUmber <= 150
```

Had we used the OR (| |) logical operator, the output would have come out as true.

Just to remind you, the >= operator means greater than or equal to. It is > for greater than, or it is < for less than. Take some time to play around your logical or relational operators because this is one of the main pillars of computer science.

Type Test Operators

The as, is, and is! operators are handy for checking types at runtime.

Consider this code:

```
//code 1.41
main(List<String> arguments) {
  int myNumber = 13;
  bool isTrue = true;
  print(myNumber is int);
  print(myNumber is! int);
  print(myNumber is! bool);
  print(myNumber is bool);
}
```

The first one is true, the second one is false, and so on.

```
//output
true
false
true
false
```

Assignment Operators

While assigning a value, we use the = operator. What happens when the assigned-to variable is null? We use a special type of operator: - ??=.

Consider this code:

```
//code 1.42
main(List<String> arguments) {
  int firstNum = 10;
  int secondNum;
  if(firstNum == 10) print("The value of ${firstNum} is set.");
  if (secondNum == null) print("It is true.");
  secondNum ??= firstNum;
  print(secondNum);
}
```

Now look at the output:

```
//output
The value of 10 is set.
It is true.
10
```

In code 1.42, we have assigned the value of firstNum to 10, and the type is an integer. So, we can say, the value of firstNum is set. At the same time, we have not assigned any value to secondNum, so by default, it is null. After that, we assign the integer to the variable that held null by this special operator: ??=.

Almost the same thing happens in the case of compound assignment operators. Now we are going to write the previous code in this way:

```
//code 1.43
main(List<String> arguments) {
  int firstNum = 10;
```

```
  int secondNum;
  if(firstNum == 10) print("The value of ${firstNum} is set.");
  if (secondNum == null) print("It is true.");
  secondNum ??= firstNum;
  print(secondNum);
  print("After using an assignment operator, the value changes.");
  secondNum += secondNum;
  print(secondNum);
  print("After using an assignment operator, the value changes
  again.");
  secondNum -= secondNum;
  print(secondNum);
  if (secondNum == null) print("It is true.");
  else print("it is false, because the 'secondNUm' has the
  value of ${secondNum} now.");
}
```

Look at this output where it is evident that we have changed the value of secondNum consecutively:

```
//output
The value of 10 is set.
It is true.
10

After using an assignment operator, the value changes.
20

After using an assignment operator, the value changes again.
0

it is false, because the 'secondNUm' has the value of 0 now.
```

As we progress, you will see more examples of operators.

Summary

Numbers, strings, and Booleans—they are all literals in Dart. Consider these literals: 1, 2.3, "Some Strings", true, false.

We need to remember a few things, such as the following:

```
var isValid = true;
```

- var is the data type.

- isValid is the variable name (or spot in memory).

- true is a literal.

You can mention the data type of a variable as int, double, String, or bool. If you don't, you can simply refer to them as var. In that case, when it's not mentioned, the data type is inferred.

String interpolation is a good practice. Don't use the + sign to add two strings.

Use an expression for operators, such as ${number1 + number2}.

What will be your choice? final or const? It is a difficult choice. You need to remember a few things: when you choose final, it is initialized, and when it is accessed, the memory is allocated for it. The const is implicitly final; this means when it is compiled, it is initialized, and the memory is allocated for it.

CHAPTER 2

Flow Control and Looping

Controlling the flow of your code is important. Programmers want to control the logic of their code for many reasons; one of the main reasons is that the user of the software should have many options open to them.

You may not know the conditions beforehand, in which way your programming logic should move, though. You can only guess, so as a developer, you should open as many avenues for the user as possible. There are several techniques you can adopt to control the flow of the code. For example, the if-else logic is popular.

if-else

Let's look at a simple example of controlling the flow of the code. After that, we will delve deep into the logical consequences of this approach. An if can be followed by else if the Boolean statement tested by the if block comes out as false.

```
if(it is true){
The program executes
}
Else {
This block will not execute then
}
```

© Sanjib Sinha 2020
S. Sinha, *Quick Start Guide to Dart Programming*,
https://doi.org/10.1007/978-1-4842-5562-9_2

Just the opposite happens when the expression tested by if is false.

```
if(it is false){
The program will not execute
}
Else {
This block will execute then
}
```

In programming, this testing mechanism depends on a variety of relationships. In the previous chapter, you saw some of them. You will see more here.

```
//code 2.1main(List<String> arguments) {
  bool firstButtonTouch = true;
  bool secondButtonTouch = false;
  bool thirdButtonTouch = true;
  bool fourthButtonTouch = false;

  if(firstButtonTouch) print("The giant starts running.");
  else print("To stop the giant please touch the second button.");

  if(secondButtonTouch) print("The giant stops.");
  else print("You have not touched the second button.");

  print("Touch any button to start the game.");

  if(thirdButtonTouch) print("The giant goes to sleep.");
  else print("You have not touched any button.");

  if(fourthButtonTouch) print("The giant wakes up.");
  else print("You have not touched any button.");
}
```

```
//output of code 21
The giant starts running.
You have not touched the second button.
Touch any button to start the game.
The giant goes to sleep.
You have not touched any button.
```

Now you can make this small code snippet more complicated, as shown here:

```
//code 2.2
main(List<String> arguments) {
  bool firstButtonTouch = true;
  var firstButtonUntouch;
  bool secondButtonTouch = false;
  bool thirdButtonTouch = true;
  bool fourthButtonTouch = false;
  firstButtonUntouch ??= firstButtonTouch;
  firstButtonUntouch = false;

  if (firstButtonUntouch == false || firstButtonTouch == true)
  print("The giant is sleeping.");
  else print("You need to wake up the giant. Touch the first
  button.");

  if(firstButtonTouch == true && firstButtonUntouch == false)
  print("The giant starts running.");
  print("To stop the giant please touch the second button.");

  if((secondButtonTouch == true && thirdButtonTouch == true)
  || fourthButtonTouch == false) print("The giant stops.");
  else print("You have not touched the second button.");

  print("Touch any button to start the game.");
```

```
if(thirdButtonTouch) print("The giant goes to sleep.");
else print("You have not touched any button.");

if(fourthButtonTouch) print("The giant wakes up.");
else print("You have not touched any button.");
}
```

Your output will vary, as shown here:

```
//output of code 2.2
The giant is sleeping.
The giant starts running.
To stop the giant please touch the second button.
The giant stops.
Touch any button to start the game.
The giant goes to sleep.
You have not touched any button.
```

For if-else logic, always remember the following golden rules. These are for the AND condition:

1. When both conditions are true, the result is true.

    ```
    statementOne = TRUE;
    statementTwo = TRUE;
    if(statementOne and statementTwo){
       the statement will execute, as it stands for TRUE
    }
    ```

2. When both conditions are false, the result is false.

    ```
    statementOne = FALSE;
    statementTwo = FALSE;
    if(statementOne and statementTwo){
       the statement will not execute, as it stands for FALSE
    }
    ```

3. When one condition is true and the other condition
    is false, the result is `false`.

```
statementOne = TRUE;
statementTwo = FALSE;
if(statementOne and statementTwo){
    the statement will not execute, as it stands for FALSE
}
```

Now here are the rules for the OR condition:

1. When one condition is true or one condition is false,
    the result is `true`.

```
statementOne = TRUE;
statementTwo = FALSE;
if(statementOne or statementTwo){
    the statement will execute, as it stands for TRUE
}
```

2. When both conditions are false, the result is `false`.

```
statementOne = FALSE;
statementTwo = FALSE;
if(statementOne or statementTwo){
    the statement will not execute, as it stands for
    FALSE
}
```

You should now have an idea of how you can use `if-else` logic when you need it. It can become complex when you start adding relational operators.

Finally, before leaving this section, I will show you another code snippet where the existing set of rules or principles has been changed. Rearranging the order of the AND and OR logic will give you an idea of how the output can change.

```
//code 2.3
main(List<String> arguments) {
  bool firstButtonTouch = true;
  var firstButtonUntouch;
  bool secondButtonTouch = false;
  bool thirdButtonTouch = true;
  bool fourthButtonTouch = false;
  firstButtonUntouch ??= firstButtonTouch;
  firstButtonUntouch = false;

  if (firstButtonUntouch == false || firstButtonTouch == true)
  print("The giant is sleeping.");
  else if (thirdButtonTouch) print("You need to wake up the
  giant. Touch the first button.");
  else if(firstButtonTouch == true && firstButtonUntouch ==
  false) print("The giant starts running.");
  else if (secondButtonTouch) print("To stop the giant please
  touch the second button.");
  else if((secondButtonTouch == true && thirdButtonTouch
  == true) || fourthButtonTouch == false) print("The giant
  stops.");
  else if (thirdButtonTouch) print("You have not touched the
  second button.");
  else if (secondButtonTouch) print("Touch any button to start
  the game.");
  else if(thirdButtonTouch) print("The giant goes to sleep.");
  else if (firstButtonUntouch) print("You have not touched any
  button.");

  if(fourthButtonTouch) print("The giant wakes up.");
  else print("You have not touched any button.");
}
```

Here is the output of the previous code:

```
The giant is sleeping.
You have not touched any button.
You can change the pattern and see what happens.
```

Let's consider the first line of code, shown here:

```
if (firstButtonUntouch == false || firstButtonTouch == true)
print("The giant is sleeping.");
```

firstButtonUntouch was initially NULL. After that we used the special ??= operator and assigned its value to firstButtonTouch, which was initially true. Therefore, firstButtonUntouch is now true. Now the set of axioms between false or true? It comes out true. And we have the output.

Conditional Expressions

Dart has two conditional expressions that can replace the if-else clause when testing small expressions. Consider this code:

```
//condition? exp1 : exp2;
int num1 = 20;
int num2 = 30;
int smallerNumber = num1 < num2? num1 : num2;
// it is expected that num1 will always be smaller
```

Here we compare num1 to num2. If num1 is smaller (num1 < num2 is true), we assign num1 to the variable. If num1 < num2 is false, we assign num2. The general form is as follows, where expression1 is returned if condition is true and expression2 is returned if condition is false:

```
condition? expression1 : expression2
```

The other form deals with `nulls`.

```
int smallNumber = num1 ?? num2";
```

If `num1` is not `null`, we assign it to `smallNumber`. If it is `null`, we assign `num2` to `smallNumber`.

Looking at Looping

In computer programming, when we need to repeat a given section of code a certain number of times until a particular condition is met, we use a *loop*. This is a control structure that is repeated until a certain condition is met.

for Loop

The general syntax of the `for` loop looks like this:

```
for(var x = 0; x <= 10; x++){
  //iteration from 0 to 10 happens in between
}
```

In the previous code, the value of x starts at 0. Then we test if the loop is going to execute (x <= 10;). If that expression returns `true`, the loop executes, and we carry out the last instruction in the `for` clause (x++), adding 1 to x. The `for` loop then tests to see whether it should run again; if it does, then x++ runs again too. This continues until x <= 10 returns `false`.

The `for` loop is necessary for iterating any collections of data. Here is a typical example of the `for` loop:

```
//code 2.4
main(List<String> arguments) {
  var proverb = StringBuffer('As Dark as a Dungeon.');
```

```
for(var x = 0; x <= 10; x++){
  proverb.write("!");
  print(proverb);
}
}
```

In the previous code, we used two built-in functions.

They are StringBuffer() and write(). We get these from Dart libraries.

The output is as follows:

```
//output of code 2.4
As Dark as a Dungeon.!
As Dark as a Dungeon.!!
As Dark as a Dungeon.!!!
As Dark as a Dungeon.!!!!
As Dark as a Dungeon.!!!!!
As Dark as a Dungeon.!!!!!!
As Dark as a Dungeon.!!!!!!!
As Dark as a Dungeon.!!!!!!!!
As Dark as a Dungeon.!!!!!!!!!
As Dark as a Dungeon.!!!!!!!!!!
As Dark as a Dungeon.!!!!!!!!!!!
```

In our future discussions, we will use the for loop quite extensively, so currently, let's stop here. You should understand the concept of why the exclamatory sign has increased from 0 to 10. It stops when the certain condition (here x=10) is met.

I am now going to cover an interesting feature of iterating collections, namely, using Set and Map. When the object you are going to iterate is Iterable, you can use the forEach() method. We are about to present two sets of collections; one is Set, and the other is Map.

```
//code 2.5
main(List<String> arguments) {
  Set mySet = {1, 2, 3};
  var myProducts = {
    1 : 'TV',
    2 : 'Refrigerator',
    3 : mySet.lookup(2),
    4 : 'Tablet',
    5 : 'Computer'
  };
  var userCollection = {"name": "John Smith", 'Email':
  'john@sanjib.site'};

  myProducts.forEach((x, y) => print("${x} : ${y}"));
  userCollection.forEach((k,v) => print('${k}: ${v}'));
}
```

As you see in the previous code, there are two sets, myProducts and userCollection. In both sets, a key=>value pair is declared. In the first case, 1 is key, and TV is the value. Now, Dart has a built-in forEach(key:value) method that can be used to give the output. In the first instance, x is the key, and y represents the value. After that, we use string interpolation to give the output.

Here is the output:

```
//output of code 2.5
1 : TV
2 : Refrigerator
3 : 2
4 : Tablet
5 : Computer
name: John Smith
Email: john@sanjib.site
```

When you do not know the current iteration counter, the `forEach()` method is a good option. In usual cases, `Iterable` classes, such as `List` and `Set`, also support the `for()` loop form of iteration.

Consider this code:

```
//code 2.6
main(List<String> arguments) {
  var myCollection = [1, 2, 3, 4];

  for(var x in myCollection){
    print("${x}");
  }
}
```

Here is the output:

```
//output of code 2.6
1
2
3
4
```

while and do-while

On a given Boolean condition, the `while` loop controls the flow and repeatedly executes the value. It loops through a block of code, as long as the specified condition is `true`.

Consider this simple example to understand the structure:

```
while (condition) {
  // code block to be executed
}
```

Here's a simple example that prints out from 0 to 10:

```
int x = 0;
while (x <= 10) {
  print("The output: ${x}");
  x++;
}
```

I hope you can see the similarity between the for and while loops. The syntactical structure is just different.

Be careful about handling the while loop. Since a while loop evaluates the condition before the loop, you must know how to stop the loop at the right time before it enters into infinity.

```
//code 2.7
main(List<String> arguments) {
  var num = 5;
  var factorial = 1;
  print("The value of the variable 'num' is decreasing this
  way:");

  while(num >=1) {
    factorial = factorial * num;
    num--;
    print("'=>' ${num}");
  }
  print("The factorial  is ${factorial}");
}
```

In the previous code, before the loop begins, the while loop evaluates the condition. Since the value of the variable num is 5 and it is greater than or equal to 1, the condition is true. So, the loop begins. As the loop begins, we have also kept reducing the value of the variable num; otherwise, it would have entered into an infinite loop.

The value of the variable reduces this way:

```
//output of code 2.8
The value of the variable 'num' is decreasing this way:
'=>' 4
'=>' 3
'=>' 2
'=>' 1
'=>' 0
The factorial is 120
```

In the case of a do-while loop, it evaluates the condition after the loop.

```
//code 2.9
main(List<String> arguments) {
  var num = 5;
  var factorial = 1;

  do {
    factorial = factorial * num;
    num--;
    print("The value of the variable 'num' is decreasing to :
    ${num}");
    print("The factorial  is ${factorial}");
  }
  while(num >=1);
}
```

We have slightly changed the code snippet so that it will show the reducing value of the variable, and at the same time it will show you how the value of the factorial increases.

```
//output of code 2.10
The value of the variable 'num' is decreasing to : 4
The factorial  is 5
```

```
The value of the variable 'num' is decreasing to : 3
The factorial   is 20
The value of the variable 'num' is decreasing to : 2
The factorial   is 60
The value of the variable 'num' is decreasing to : 1
The factorial   is 120
The value of the variable 'num' is decreasing to : 0
The factorial   is 120
```

Once you understand the pattern of loops, you can easily choose between for, while, and do-while. Let's look at that now.

Patterns in Looping

I have met many students who feel confused about the while loop. I cover the looping structure in this section so that you can understand it.

People often do not know that a for loop can also turn into an infinite loop if it is not handled properly.

Actually, some concepts of loops are the same for every loop, be it for, while, or do-while. There are three things to remember.

- Counter variable

- Condition checking

- According to the condition, increment or decrement

Let's consider the code snippet:

```
void forLoopFunction(){
  for(var i = 0; i <= 5; i ++){
    print(i);
  }
}
```

```
void whileLoopFunction (){
  var i = 0;
  while(i <= 5){
    print(i);
    i++;
  }
}
// in doWhileLoop the execution part comes before the specified
condition. The concept is same.
void doWhileLoopFunction (){
  var i = 0;
  do{
    print(i);
    i++;
  } while(i <= 5);
}

main(){
  //print(smallerNumber);
  //print(smallNumber);
  forLoopFunction();
  print("");
  whileLoopFunction();
  print("");
  doWhileLoopFunction();
}
```

Here is the output:

```
0
1
2
3
```

4

5

0

1

2

3

4

5

0

1

2

3

4

5

Let's consider the for loop first.

```
for(var i = 0; i <= 5; i ++){
  print(i);
}
```

We have started with the counter variable, here i = 0. Then we have checked the condition, as shown here:

```
i <= 5
```

After the second step, we have incremented the value: i++.

The steps are quite logical. We could not have decremented the value. It would have taken us to an infinite loop because after starting at 0, the value of i would decrease, and the specified condition would remain true forever. If we had decremented the value of i, by writing i--, the condition checking would have never stopped until our computer's memory permitted. A hang or freeze occurs when the program ceases to respond to code.

Now we have done the same thing in the while loop. The steps are just a little bit different.

```
var i = 0;
while(i <= 5){
  print(i);
  i++;
}
```

In the previous code, the counter variable comes before the while loop starts. The while loop starts with the condition checking, as shown here:

```
i <= 5
```

We saw the same thing in the second step of the for loop. After that, according to the condition, we incremented the value of i inside the while loop. Once the value of i equals 6, it immediately stops responding to the inputs. It gives output from 0 to 5.

Now let's look at the do-while loop code. We start with the counter variable, and then we increment or decrement the value.

```
var i = 0;
do{
  print(i);
  i++;
} while(i <= 5);
```

In the last stage, we check the condition inside the while loop.

You may ask which loop is better. Actually, it depends on the context. In some situations, the for loop is enough. In fact, in most cases, we can manage with the for loop. If we want to know how many times a given number can be divided by 2 before it is less than or equal to 1, the while loop is better to use.

for Loop Labels

In some situations, we use nested for loops. Inside a for loop, we can run another for loop; and in many cases, this is essential. In Dart, there is a concept called a *label* that allows us to handle the outer loop and the inner loop separately. With the help of continue and break, we can jump to labels. Let's look at the code first; after that, I will explain what is happening:

```
void labelsLoop (){
  outerloop: for(var x = 1; x <= 3; x++){
    print("One cycle of outerloop with $x starts and the whole
    innerloop runs.");

    innerloop: for(var y = 1; y <= 3; y++){
      if(x == 1 && y == 1){
        print("Since outerloop $x and innerloop $y both are 1,
        it gives no output.");
        break innerloop;
      }
      print(y);
    }

    print("One cycle of outerloop ends with $x");
  }
}
main(List<String> arguments){
  labelsLoop();
}
```

If you look at the output shown here, you can understand how it works:

```
One cycle of the outer loop with 1 starts and the whole inner
loop runs.
Since outer loop 1 and inner loop 1 both are 1, it gives no
output.
```

One cycle of the outer loop ends with 1
One cycle of the outer loop with 2 starts and the whole inner
loop runs.
1
2
3
One cycle of the outer loop ends with 2
One cycle of the outer loop with 3 starts and the whole inner
loop runs.
1
2
3
One cycle of the outer loop ends with 3

We can also use break in normal cases, without a label.

Consider this code:

```
void main() {
  for (var j = 0; j < 5; j++) {
        if (j > 3 ) break ;
    print(j);
  }
}
```

Here is the output:

```
0
1
2
3
```

As you see in the previous code, where we have used labels, the counter variable, condition checking, and increment parts are the same in both the outer loop and the inner loop. So when the outer loop starts with 1, the inner loop inside the outer loop also starts with 1, and it should have completed the whole cycle. But we have injected an if statement and told the program that when the value of the outer loop and the inner loop both are 1, break the inner loop. We have used the labels outerloop and innerloop to demarcate the loops. Using the if statement, that particular cycle of innerloop could not complete the whole cycle. However, after that, it goes on as usual.

A label is a distinctive concept of Dart.

Continue with the for Loop

You have just seen how we have explicitly broken the inner loop and stopped one cycle of the inner loop. So, break is an important concept while using the for loop. At the same time, the continue keyword also plays a key role in the for loop.

Let's consider this code snippet:

```
void loopContinue(){
  for(var num = 1; num <= 5; num++){
    if(num % 2 == 0 ){
      print("These are all even numbers. $num");
      continue;
    } print("These are all odd numbers. $num");
  }
}
main(List<String> arguments){
  loopContinue();
}
```

Take a look at the output, and you will understand how the keyword continue works. It takes us out of the current loop to the start of the next one.

```
These are all odd numbers. 1
These are all even numbers. 2
These are all odd numbers. 3
These are all even numbers. 4
These are all odd numbers. 5
```

break and continue are two important concepts not only in Dart but in every programming language.

Decision-Making with switch and case

In some cases, decision-making can be easier when you use switch instead of if-else logic. switch statements in Dart compare integers, strings, or compile-time constants using the double equal sign (==) behind the scenes; it maintains the rule, though, that the compared objects must be instances of the same class and not of any of its subtypes. (Don't worry, this will become clear when we get to classes later in the book.)

Consider this simple example first:

```
void main() {
   var marks = "A";
   switch(marks) {
      case "A": {  print("Very Good"); }
      break;

      case "B": {  print("Good"); }
      break;

      case "C": {  print("Fair"); }
      break;

      case "D": {  print("Poor"); }
      break;
```

```
    default: { print("Fail"); }
    break;
  }
}
```

The output is Very Good. Here the object marks is of the same class as in the case statements (String).

Let's look at another example:

```
//code 2.11
main(List<String> arguments) {
  //that could be the input value that would take inputs from
  users
  var startingTime = 5;
  switch (startingTime) {
    case 5:
      print("Printer Ready");
      break;
    case 6:
      print("Start printing");
      break;
    case 7:
      print("Stop for a second");
      break;
    case 8:
      print("Loading a tray and roll the paper.");
      break;
    case 9:
      print("Printer Ready, start printing.");
      break;
```

```
  default:
    print("Default ${startingTime}");
  }
}
```

The significance of break is that if the condition is met, the switch statement ends, and the program continues.

When someone starts the printer, it gives us output like this because startingTime is 5:

```
//output of code 2.11
Printer Ready
```

We have used a default clause to execute the code when no case clause matches.

Summary

Controlling the flow of code is essential for many reasons. This is the foundation of any algorithms that instruct computers to behave in a certain way. Building a mobile or web application needs many such instructions. Because these algorithms can be complex, they require an understanding of a few other key concepts such as functions and object-oriented programming.

In the next chapter, we will talk about functions first. After that, you will learn object-oriented programming thoroughly, and we will then return to the topic of features to discuss other key features of them.

CHAPTER 3

Functions and Objects

When we say functions are objects in Dart, it may seem confusing if you're a beginner. Basically, because Dart is an object-oriented language, even functions are objects and have a type called Function.

This means many things. First, you can assign a function to a variable, and you can even pass a function as an argument to other functions. You can also call an instance of a Dart class as if it were a function.

In this chapter, first you will now learn how a Dart function works. Then you will learn about objects. To understand objects, you need to have an understanding of object-oriented programming, which we'll also talk about in this chapter.

Functions

Let's see how functions work. This section is a basic introduction, and I will cover this topic more in-depth later when discussing methods in object-oriented programming.

© Sanjib Sinha 2020
S. Sinha, *Quick Start Guide to Dart Programming*,
https://doi.org/10.1007/978-1-4842-5562-9_3

Before writing a function, you need to remember these major points:

- It is a good practice to define the type of a function. So, type annotation is recommended.

- Although Dart recommends type annotation, a function still works without any type declaration. In other words, you can omit the type and write it straight. Dart uses type interference. Here's an example:

```
Map<String, dynamic> arguments = {'John': 'Smith',
'Chicago': 42};
Alternatively, you can use var and let Dart infer the
type:
var arguments = {'John': 'Smith', 'Chicago': 42};
// Map<String, Object>
```

- However, the most important thing to remember in Dart is that whatever value you want to return from a function, you need to change the type of that function accordingly. If you want an integer value to return, for example, you should change the type of the function to integer.

- Simply put, for void, nothing is returned from a function. So, whenever you use the keyword void before the function, you need to use print(object) to see what's happening inside that function.

The following are two simple functions with type annotations, and we have called them inside the main() function:

```
//code 3.1
main(List<String> arguments) {
  isTrue();
  isFalse();
}
```

```
void isTrue(){
  print("It's true.");
}
void isFalse(){
  print("It's false.");
}

//output of code 3.1
It's true.
It's false.
```

Let's omit the type and see how the same code works.

```
//code 3.2
main(List<String> arguments) {
  isTrue();
  isFalse();
}
isTrue(){
  print("It's true.");
}
isFalse(){
  print("It's false.");
}
```

This gives us the same result because according to the type of the value, it is automatically inferred. Here Dart knows they, here the types, are void because we are not using any return statements.

So, type annotations do not matter in such cases, but for API building (we will cover this part at the end of this book), type annotation is necessary.

Note   If you change this code by adding the type bool before the function name, it still works without giving any error. Dart just uses what you've written because there is no reason to display an error (we're not trying to return something that is not a bool). It's loose like that.

You can call another function inside a function, as shown here:

```
//code 3.3
main(List<String> arguments) {
  myName();
}
myName(){
  print("My name is John");
  myAge(12);
}
myAge(int age){
  print("My age is ${age}");
}
```

Later inside the function myName(), we have passed the age parameter or argument and get this output:

```
//output of code 3.3
My name is John
My age is 12
```

So, that was a short introduction to functions; it is evident that a function plays the same role that the verb plays in human languages. It is the action part of programming. You will understand it better when we discuss methods in object-oriented programming later in this chapter.

Before leaving this section, let look at another piece of code where we actually return a value, so the return type is important. We also use a different function syntax called *fat arrow*.

```
void withoutReturningValue(){
  print("We cannot return any value from this function.");
}

int anIntegerReturnTypeFunction(){
  int num = 10;
  return num;
}
//using Fat Arrow
String stringReturnTypeFunction(String name, String address) =>
"This is $name and this is $address and we have used the Fat
Arrow method.";

main(){
  withoutReturningValue();
  var returningInteger = anIntegerReturnTypeFunction();
  print("We are returning an integer: $returningInteger");
  print(stringReturnTypeFunction("John", "Jericho Town"));
}
```

First we use int as the return type of anIntegerReturnTypeFunction() and use the return keyword to specify the int that we're returning. This value is then assigned to a variable in main().

Using the fat arrow method, we can return a value from a function in one line. This time we say it returns a String type. We will see more instances of fat arrow syntax later in the chapter.

The final type of function we should look at is the recursive function, shown here:

```
int getRecurse(int num)
{
    if (num > 1)
        return num * getRecurse(num - 1);
    else return 1;
}

main()
{
  print(getRecurse(5));
}
```

You can see that in main() we call getRecurse() with an int parameter of 5. Inside getRecurse(), we have an if clause to control the number of times we recurse. If the parameter is greater than 1, the code multiplies the parameter by the results of another call to getRecurse, with 1 subtracted from the parameter. This recursive call is repeated until the parameter equals 1. At that stage, the chain of recursion is wound up, and the final result is returned.

You can add some print statements to see the recursion in action.

```
int getRecurse(int num)
{
  if (num > 1) {
    print("In getRecurse and num is $num");
    return num * getRecurse(num - 1);
  } else return 1;
}
```

```
main()
{
  print(getRecurse(5));
}
```

The output is as follows:

```
In getRecurse and num is 5
In getRecurse and num is 4
In getRecurse and num is 3
In getRecurse and num is 2
120
```

You can see how $5 \times 4 \times 3 \times 2$ is 120, the final line of output.

Objects

As you know, Dart is an object-oriented language, which means it has classes and objects.

Let's start with a simple class and an object. So far you have seen variables and functions. Let's think about something that will hold variables and functions. We call it a *class*.

Suppose we have a Car class that has three properties: name, model number, and whether it is turned on. It has also two methods (outside the object-oriented paradigm we call them *functions*) called turnOn(bool) and isTurnedOn(). Consider these the "action" parts of the class Car. When we pass the bool value true to turnOn(), the car starts, and when we pass the bool value false, the car stops.

Now imagine a manufacturer wants to build many cars that have separate names and model numbers but each one has one method called turnOn(bool). In this scenario, each car is an object or instance of the Car class.

Consider the following code:

```
//code 3.4
main(List<String> arguments) {
  var newCar = new Car();
  newCar.carName = "Red Angel";
  newCar.carModel = 256;
  newCar.turnOn(false);

  if(newCar.isTurnedOn()){
    print("${newCar.carName} starts. It has model number
    ${newCar.carModel}");
  } else print("${newCar.carName} stops. It has model number
  ${newCar.carModel}");
}

class Car {
  int carModel = 123;
  String carName = "Blue Angel";
  bool isOn = true;

  bool turnOn(bool turnOn){
    isOn = turnOn;
  }

  bool isTurnedOn() {
    return isOn;
  }
}
```

It gives us this output:

```
//output of code 3.4
Red Angel stops. It has model number 256
```

Look at the Car class. It has three properties or attributes: carName, carModel, and isOn. We treat them as variables, but since they are inside a class, we will call them *properties*, *members*, or *attributes*. These values can be changed when we create an instance. In fact, we have done this inside the main() function. The default values were 123, Blue Angel, and true. But we have some output where the name changes to Red Angel, the model has been changed to 256, and the car stops. We have created an instance or object of the Car class by simply writing this line:

```
var newCar = new Car();
```

Next , we have defined the name and the model number as follows:

```
newCar.carName = "Red Angel";
newCar.carModel = 256;
```

The next step is vital, because we check that the method isTurnedOn() returns true.

```
if(newCar.isTurnedOn()){
  print("${newCar.carName} starts. It has model number
  ${newCar.carModel}");
} else print("${newCar.carName} stops. It has model number
${newCar.carModel}");
```

Now according to our logic, if this is true, the car should start. But in the output, we have seen that it stops.

Why does this happen?

It happens because in our Car class, we have already set that value as false.

Let's change it to true, as shown here:

```
//code 3.5
main(List<String> arguments) {
  var newCar = new Car();
```

```
  newCar.carName = "Red Angel";
  newCar.carModel = 256;
  newCar.turnOn(true);

  if(newCar.isTurnedOn()){
    print("${newCar.carName} starts. It has model number
    ${newCar.carModel}");
  } else print("${newCar.carName} stops. It has model number
  ${newCar.carModel}");
}

class Car {
  int carModel = 123;
  String carName = "Blue Angel";
  bool isOn = true;

  bool turnOn(bool turnOn){
    isOn = turnOn;
  }

  bool isTurnedOn() {
    return isOn;
  }
}
```

Take a look at the output again:

```
//output of code 3.5
Red Angel starts. It has model number 256
```

From this example, we can conclude one thing: a class is a blueprint of an object. An object or an instance of a class is extremely powerful; it is not like simple variables, holding one reference to a spot in the memory where we can store only a value. Through an app object we can run a large complicated application; moreover, we can make a complex layer of logic behind an object.

Digging Deep into Object-Oriented Programming

In the previous code, you saw these lines of code where we have used (.) notation to get the value of Car class members:

```
if(newCar.isTurnedOn()){
  print("${newCar.carName} starts. It has model number
  ${newCar.carModel}");
} else print("${newCar.carName} stops. It has model number
${newCar.carModel}");
```

We actually used the class members.

When we use a (.) notation, we usually refer to object properties or methods. A class may have properties and methods. After all, it is a blueprint of how an object will behave. How an object will behave in the future depends on the class that has already been written.

Whether a car object will start or stop depends on that blueprint.

So, we can say that objects have members consisting of functions and data; when you call a method, you actually invoke it on an object.

Let's see some more examples to get acquainted with the idea of classes and objects. To start, let's assume a father bear is eating six fish. To create the object of father bear, we need to have a bear class first where we have one member property for "number of fish" and one member method for "eating that number of fish." Ideally, both the property and the method should be annotated with the type int.

```
//code 3.6
class Bear {
  int eatFish(int numberOfFish){
    return numberOfFish;
  }
}
```

```
main(List<String> arguments){
  var fatherBear = new Bear();
  print("Father bear eats ${fatherBear.eatFish(6)} number of
  fish.");
}
```

That's a very simple program. We get this output:

```
//output of code 3.6
Father bear eats 6 number of fish.
```

Can we take this code to the next level? As father bear eats fish and sleeps for some hours, he gains weight. Consider this code:

```
//code 3.7
class Bear {
  int numberOfFish;
  int hourOfSleep;
  int weightGain;

  int eatFish(int numberOfFish){
    return numberOfFish;
  }

  int sleepAfterEatingFish(int hourOfSleep){
    return hourOfSleep;
  }

  int weightGaining(int numberOfFish, int hourOfSleep){
    weightGain = numberOfFish * hourOfSleep;
    return weightGain;
  }
}
```

```
main(List<String> arguments){
  var fatherBear = new Bear();
  fatherBear.numberOfFish = 6;
  fatherBear.hourOfSleep = 10;
  print("Father bear eats ${fatherBear.eatFish(fatherBear.
  numberOfFish)} number of fish. And he sleeps for ${fatherBear.
  sleepAfterEatingFish(fatherBear.hourOfSleep)} hours.");
  print("Father bear has gained ${fatherBear.
  weightGaining(fatherBear.numberOfFish, fatherBear.
  hourOfSleep)} pounds of weight.");
}
```

In the previous code, we have added a few things, such as hourOfSleep and weightGain; further, we have added two related methods: sleepAfterEatingFish() and weightGaining(). As you see, we have passed two related parameters through those methods.

Father bear sleeps after eating the fish and gains weight. The value of the weight he gains comes from the multiplication of hourOfSleep and numberOfFish.

So, we get this output while running this small program:

```
//output of code 3.7
Father bear eats 6 number of fish. And he sleeps for 10 hours.
Father bear has gained 60 pounds of weight.
```

Dart is an extremely flexible language. You can write the same code in fewer lines that used in other languages. You do not have to use the typical curly braces, and you can even omit the return keyword to return the value automatically. You can also omit the new word to create an instance. We are going to write the same code in this way now:

```
//code 3.8
class Bear {
  int numberOfFish;
```

```
  int hourOfSleep;
  int weightGain;
  //changing the styles of the methods completely
  int eatFish(int numberOfFish) => numberOfFish;
  int sleepAfterEatingFish(int hourOfSleep) => hourOfSleep;
  int weightGaining(int numberOfFish, int hourOfSleep) =>
  weightGain = numberOfFish * hourOfSleep;
}

main(List<String> arguments){
  var fatherBear = Bear(); //omitted the 'new' word
  fatherBear.numberOfFish = 7;
  fatherBear.hourOfSleep = 20;
    print("Father bear eats ${fatherBear.eatFish(fatherBear.
    numberOfFish)} fishes. And he sleeps for ${fatherBear.
    sleepAfterEatingFish(fatherBear.hourOfSleep)} hours.");
  print("Father bear has gained ${fatherBear.
  weightGaining(fatherBear.numberOfFish, fatherBear.
  hourOfSleep)} pounds of weight.");
}
```

We have slightly changed the value of hours and the number of fish. The output also changes, as shown here:

```
//output of code 3.8
Father bear eats 7 fishes. And he sleeps for 20 hours.
Father bear has gained 140 pounds of weight.
```

To make our life easier, in object-oriented programming there is a concept called a *constructor*. Whenever you create an instance or object with or without the new keyword, inside the class a method is automatically called. This method is called the *constructor method*. In the next section, we will explore the concept of constructors.

Examining Constructors

The foremost task of constructors is to create objects. Whenever we try to create an object and write this line:

```
var fatherBear = Bear();
```

we are actually trying to arrange a spot in the memory for that object. The real work begins when we connect that spot with class properties and methods.

Using a constructor, we can do that job more efficiently because constructors come first when we instantiate. Not only that, Dart allows us to create more than one constructor, which is a great advantage.

Let's write our Bear class in a new way by using a constructor:

```
//code 3.9
class Bear {
  int numberOfFish;
  int hourOfSleep;
  int weightGain;

  Bear(this.numberOfFish, this.hourOfSleep );// Constructor

  int eatFish(int numberOfFish) => numberOfFish;
  int sleepAfterEatingFish(int hourOfSleep) => hourOfSleep;
  int weightGaining(int numberOfFish, int hourOfSleep) =>
  weightGain = numberOfFish * hourOfSleep;
}

main(List<String> arguments){
  var fatherBear = Bear(6, 10);
    print("Father bear eats ${fatherBear.eatFish(fatherBear.
    numberOfFish)} fishes. And he sleeps for ${fatherBear.
    sleepAfterEatingFish(fatherBear.hourOfSleep)} hours.");
```

```
print("Father bear has gained ${fatherBear.weightGaining
(fatherBear.numberOfFish, fatherBear.hourOfSleep)} pounds of
weight.");
}
```

Creating a constructor is extremely easy. Look at this line:

```
Bear(this.numberOfFish, this.hourOfSleep);
```

The same class name works as a method, and we have passed two arguments through that method. Once we get those values, we calculate the third variable for the weight gain. In a later section of this chapter of the book we will talk more about constructors.

Now it gets easier to pass the two values while creating the object. We have used the this keyword. The this keyword represents an implicit object pointing to the current class object.

We could have done the same thing by creating a constructor in this way, which is more traditional:

```
//code 3.10
class Bear {
  int numberOfFish;
  int hourOfSleep;
  int weightGain;

  Bear(int numOfFish, int hourOfSleep ){// constructor
    this  .numberOfFish = numOfFish  ;//using this keyword to
                                        point out the current
                                        class object
    this  .hourOfSleep = hourOfSleep;
  }
  //Bear(this.numberOfFish, this.hourOfSleep);
```

```
  int eatFish(int numberOfFish) => numberOfFish;
  int sleepAfterEatingFish(int hourOfSleep) => hourOfSleep;
  int weightGaining(int numberOfFish, int hourOfSleep) =>
  weightGain = numberOfFish * hourOfSleep;
}

main(List<String> arguments){
  var fatherBear = Bear(6, 10);
  print("Father bear eats ${fatherBear.eatFish(fatherBear.
  numberOfFish)} fishes. And he sleeps for ${fatherBear.
  sleepAfterEatingFish(fatherBear.hourOfSleep)} hours.");
  print("Father bear has gained ${fatherBear.
  weightGaining(fatherBear.numberOfFish, fatherBear.
  hourOfSleep)} pounds of weight.");
}
```

In both cases, the output is the same as before:

```
//output of code 3.10
Father bear eats 6 fishes. And he sleeps for 10 hours.
Father bear has gained 60 pounds of weight.
```

In the previous code, you can even get the object's type very easily. We can change the type of value quite easily. Watch the main() function again:

```
//code 3.11
main(List<String> arguments){
  var fatherBear = Bear(6, 10);
  fatherBear.weightGain = fatherBear.numberOfFish * fatherBear.
  hourOfSleep;
  print("Father bear eats ${fatherBear.eatFish(fatherBear.
  numberOfFish)} fishes. And he sleeps for ${fatherBear.
  sleepAfterEatingFish(fatherBear.hourOfSleep)} hours.");
```

```
print("Father bear has gained ${fatherBear.
weightGaining(fatherBear.weightGain)} pounds of weight.");
print("The type of the object : ${fatherBear.weightGain.
runtimeType}");
String weightGained = fatherBear.weightGain.toString();
print("The type of the same object has changed to :
${weightGained.runtimeType}");
}
```

Here is the output:

```
//code 3.12
main(List<String> arguments){
  var fatherBear = Bear(6, 10);
  print("Father bear eats ${fatherBear.eatFish(fatherBear.
  numberOfFish)} fishes. And he sleeps for ${fatherBear.
  sleepAfterEatingFish(fatherBear.hourOfSleep)} hours.");
  print("Father bear has gained ${fatherBear.
  weightGaining(fatherBear.numberOfFish, fatherBear.
  hourOfSleep)} pounds of weight.");
  print("The type of the object : ${fatherBear.weightGain.
  runtimeType}");
  String weightGained = fatherBear.weightGain.toString();
  print("The type of the same object has changed to :
  ${weightGained.runtimeType}");
}
```

How to Implement Classes

Now you have an idea of how classes and objects work together. A class is
a blueprint that has some instance variables and methods. A class might
have many tasks, but it is a good practice and one of the major paradigms

of object-oriented programming that a single class should have a single task. When many classes work together, they should not be tightly coupled. They should be loosely coupled.

Loosely coupled means when you use many objects from different classes, they should not be glued together. They should not affect other objects when they are affected.

This is a principle that is known as the SOLID design principle. Briefly, it means that one object should not interfere with another object. Consider a Car class, where the Wheel class should not be glued to the Steering class. That is why when we get a flat tire, we can still steer the car to a safe place. When building software applications, you should always try to decouple all classes.

In Dart, we might implement the same principle while creating classes.

Let's create a single class with a single task. We are going to create a class that will check whether a URL is secure or not.

```
//code 3.13
class CheckHTTPS {
  String urlCheck;
  CheckHTTPS(this.urlCheck);

  bool checkURL(String urlCheck){
    if(this.urlCheck.contains("https")){
      return true;
    } else return false;
  }
}
main(List<String> arguments){
  var newURL = CheckHTTPS('http://sanjib.site');
  if(!newURL.checkURL(newURL.urlCheck)) {
    print("The URL ${newURL.urlCheck} is not secured");
  }
}
```

We get this output after checking the URL:

```
//output of code 3.13
The URL http://sanjib.site is not secured
```

So, we have some basic steps to follow. Whenever we want to create a class, we should have a clear vision about what this class will do. What will be its task?

First, we need some variables. Next, we need one or more methods where we can play with these variables.

```
//code 3.14
class MyClass {
  String myVariable; //property or instance variable, initially
                        null
  MyClass(this.myVariable); //constructor

  String myMethod(){ //method declaration
    return "This is my method and this is ${myVariable}";
    //returning value
  }
}

main(List<String> arguments){
  var myObject = MyClass("My String"); //creating new instance
                                        of class MyClass
  print("${myObject.myMethod()}"); //printing the value
}
```

Look at the code: we have declared an instance variable first. It is of the String type. Since we have not initialized the variable, it is initially null. In the next step, we have constructed an object by declaring a constructor where we have passed the instance variable. Our method's type is also String. In the method, we have returned a String object.

In the main() function, we have created an object and declared the type as MyClass; and at the same time, we have passed a string value to the constructor. Finally, we have called the class method and displayed the output.

In the next section, we will write some methods and try to understand how they work. Methods are essential parts of any class because they are the action part.

Lexical Scope in Functions

This concept is extremely important as far as Dart functions are concerned.

Note   Later, when we dig deep into object-oriented programming, we will see how the concepts of access plays a vital role in Dart.

Let's return to functions. First look at the following code and read the comments:

```
//code 3.15
var outsideVariable = "I am an outsider.";

main(List<String> arguments){
  //we can access the outside variable
  print(outsideVariable);
  // we cannot access the insider variable, it gives us error
  //print(insiderVariable);
  // it is an insider function
  String insiderFunction(){
    // I can access the outside variable, no problem
    print("This is from the insider function.");
    print(outsideVariable);
```

```
    String insiderVariable = "I am an insider";
    print(insiderVariable); // it's okay to access this insider
  }
  insiderFunction();
}
```

First, we have declared a variable outside our main() function. It is called outsideVariable. We can access that variable inside the main() function as an object. Remember, everything in Dart is an object.

Second, we have declared an insider function called insiderFunction(). Now inside that insider function, we can safely call the outsider variable. In addition, if we create another insider variable, we can also call it.

So, we get this output:

```
//output of code 3.15
I am an outsider.
This is from the insider function.
I am an outsider.
I am an insider
```

As such, there is no problem regarding the output. However, it will not be the same experience if we try to call the insider variable from outside the scope of our insider function.

```
//code 3.16
var outsideVariable = "I am an outsider.";
main(List<String> arguments){
  //we can access the outside variable
  print(outsideVariable);
  // we cannot access the insider variable, it gives us error
  print(insiderVariable);
  // it is an insider function
```

```
String insiderFunction(){
  // I can access the outisde variable, no problem
  print("This is from the insider function.");
  print(outsideVariable);
  String insiderVariable = "I am an insider";
  print(insiderVariable); // it's okay to access this insider
}
insiderFunction();
}
```

Now, look at the output:

```
//output of code 3.16
bin/main.dart:11:9: Error: Getter not found: 'insiderVariable'.
  print(insiderVariable);
        ^^^^^^^^^^^^^^^
```

We should understand this "inside and outside" case.

This is called *lexical scope*. You can call an outside variable inside the main() function. However, if you define an object inside a function, you cannot call it from outside of that function.

A Few Words About Getter and Setter

Let's again return to the topic of object-oriented programming to learn about a key concept called the getter and setter. We can explicitly set a value and get it in this way, using the . notation:

```
//code 3.17
class myClass {
    String name;
    String get getName => name;
    set setName(String aValue) => name = aValue;
}
```

```
main(List<String> arguments){
  var myObject = myClass();
  myObject.setName = "Sanjib";
  print(myObject.getName);
}
```

This gives us the output Sanjib. But how does this happen? In myClass, we have defined the setName() method to accept a parameter called aValue. Later we have called that method through the instance (myObject. setName) of the class myClass. The interesting thing is that the method setName(String aValue) defined inside myClass now works as an attribute.

You may ask why we should use getter and setter when every class has been associated with a default getter and setter?

Actually, we are overriding the default value by explicitly defining the getter and setter.

Different Types of Parameters

Whether in a class method or in a function, sometimes you need to pass values. You can call them *arguments* or *parameters*, whichever you like.

Dart is flexible; it gives ample opportunity to developers to manipulate the parameters. You can use default parameters; in such cases, you need to give a value for the defaults. This is compulsory. But there are three other options available in Dart. You can use positional parameters, named parameters, and optional parameters.

The following code uses default and positional parameters:

```
//code 3.18
//default parameters
String defaultParameters(String name, String address, {int
age = 10}){
  return "$name and $address and age $age";
}
```

```
//optional parameters
String optionalParameters(String name, String address,
[int age] ){
  return "$name and $address and $age";
}

main(){
  print(defaultParameters("John", "Jericho"));
  print(optionalParameters("John", "Form Chikago"));
  // overriding the default age
  print(defaultParameters("JOhn", "Jericho", age : 20));
}
```

Inside the main() function, in our default parameter function, we have passed only two values: name and address. We did not pass the age. We did not have to, because it already was defined in our function: {int age = 10}. Remember to use the curly braces to define the default parameter.

Can we override the default parameter? Yes, we can. Look at this part inside the main() function:

```
// overriding the default age
print(defaultParameters("JOhn", "Jericho", age : 20));
```

We have overridden the default age and made it from 10 to 20.

Next, in the optional parameter function, we have made the age optional by keeping the value inside the square brackets.

```
//optional parameters
String optionalParameters(String name, String address, [int
age] ){
  return "$name and $address and $age";
}
```

Since the parameter age is optional, we can either pass it or ignore it. However, ignoring the optional parameter will set it to null. So, the output of the previous code will look like this:

```
//output of code 3.19
John and Jericho and age 10
John and Form Chikago and null
JOhn and Jericho and age 20
```

In the case of a named parameter, we can swap the values because it, using the named parameter is very flexible. Here sequence does not matter. Let's consider this code:

```
//code 3.20
//named parameter
int findTheVolume(int length, {int height, int breadth}){
  return length * height * breadth;
}

void main(){
  //sequence does not matter
  var  result1 = findTheVolume(10, height: 20, breadth: 30);
  var  result2 = findTheVolume(10, breadth: 30, height: 10);
  print(result1);
  print(result2);
}
```

In the previous code, we have placed height and breadth inside curly braces. So, they are named parameters that we can interchange while passing the values. Interchanging the value will not affect our code.

That is the advantage of named parameters.

More About Constructors

In any class, there are many types of constructors that can be used in any application. As usual, we have a default constructor. We can pass parameters through it. We also have named parameters. Let's look at the following code snippet and try to understand how they work:

```
//code 3.21
class Bear {
  //reference variable
  int collarID;
  //default and parameterized constructor
  Bear(this.collarID);
  //first named constructor
  Bear.firstNamedConstructor(this.collarID);
  //second named constructor
  Bear.secondNamedConstructor(this.collarID);
  void trackingBear() {
    String color; // local varia   print("Tracking the bear
                   with collar ID ${collarID}");
  }
}

main(List<String> arguments){
  // bear1 is reference variable
  // Bear() is object// It should be class no object I suppose
  var bear1 = Bear(1);
  bear1.trackingBear();
  var bear2 = Bear.firstNamedConstructor(2);
  bear2.trackingBear();
  var bear3 = Bear.secondNamedConstructor(3);
  bear3.trackingBear();
}
```

In the previous code, by Dart convention, when we write a class, we might have many things in place. First, we have a reference variable here: int collarID;. The variable called collarID contains a reference to an int object with a value of a Bear object.

Inside the main() function, when we create an instance, we will again have a reference variable.

```
// bear1 is reference variable
// Bear() is object
var bear1 = Bear(1);
```

We have passed the class-level reference variable collarID through the default constructor.

So, while defining a class and afterward creating an instance, we have two types of reference variable: the first is class-level reference variable, and the second one is an object-level or instance-level reference variable. If this does not make any sense, don't worry. We'll cover it in Chapter 7.

In the constructor part, we have one default and parameterized constructor, shown here:

```
//default and parameterized constructor
Bear(this.collarID);
Besides, we have two named constructors.
//first named constructor
Bear.firstNamedConstructor(this.collarID);
//second named constructor
Bear.secondNamedConstructor(this.collarID);
```

Through the named constructors, we have created three bear instances; moreover, each instance has the same functionality. Finally, when you run the code, you cannot distinguish between the behavior of the code that uses the default constructor and the code that uses the named constructors.

```
Tracking the bear with collar ID 1
Tracking the bear with collar ID 2
Tracking the bear with collar ID 3
```

In the next chapter, we will look at another important concept: inheritance.

CHAPTER 4

Inheritance and Mixins in Dart

One of the key features of object-oriented programming is that you can extend your classes. You extend a class to create another class, and the extended class is known as a *subclass*. The subclass inherits reference variables and class methods from the parent class, which is known as a *superclass*.

The properties of the parent class are inherited by the child class; because the properties from the parent class are extended to the child class, the parent class is also called the *base class*. For the same reason, the child class is known as the *derived class*, since it is inheriting the properties of the base class. This capability, known as *inheritance*, works in two ways.

First, you can create new classes from an existing class. That is called *single inheritance*. Dart does not support multiple inheritance (inheriting from more than one class). However, it supports *multilevel inheritance*. Therefore, we can conclude that Dart supports two types of inheritance.

- Single inheritance
- Multilevel inheritance

© Sanjib Sinha 2020
S. Sinha, *Quick Start Guide to Dart Programming*,
https://doi.org/10.1007/978-1-4842-5562-9_4

A First Look at Inheritance

Consider this simple example where we have extended an Animal class to a Cat class. This is an example of single inheritance.

```
//code 4.1
class Animal {
  String name = "Animal";
  Animal(){
    print("I am Animal class constructor.");
  }

  Animal.namedConstructor(){
    print("This is parent animal named constructor.");
  }

  void showName(){
    print(this.name);
  }

  void eat(){
    print("Animals eat everything depending on what type it
    is.");
  }
}

class Cat extends Animal {
  //overriding parent constructor
  //although constructors are not inherited
  Cat() : super(){
    print("I am child cat class overriding super Animal
    class.");
  }
```

```
Cat.namedCatConstructor() : super.namedConstructor(){
  print("The child cat named constructor overrides the parent
  animal named constructor.");
}

@override // method overriding
void showName(){
  print(this.name);
}

@override
void eat(){
  super.eat();
  print("Cat doesn't eat vegetables..");
}
}
main(List<String> arguments){
  var cat = Cat();
  cat.name = "Meaow";
  cat.showName();
  cat.eat();
  var anotherCat = Cat.namedCatConstructor();
}
```

Let's first look at the output; after that, we will discuss the features of subclasses and superclasses.

```
//output of code 4.1
I am Animal class constructor.
I am child cat class overriding super Animal class.
Hi from cat.
```

Animals eat everything depending on what type it is. Cat doesn't eat vegetables..

This is parent animal named constructor. The child cat named constructor overrides the parent animal named constructor.

The code is quite simple to follow; the superclass or base class Animal has two constructors: the default and a named constructor. Subclasses don't inherit constructors from their superclass. The subclass or derived class Cat overrides both constructors. You have to specify which constructor you are overriding in the subclass's constructor definition. If you do not, then your named subclass constructor will override the default constructor of the parent class.

```dart
Cat.namedCatConstructor() : super.namedConstructor(){
  print("The child cat named constructor overrides the parent
  animal named constructor.");
}
```

Now, let's change the code a little bit and follow the output. You will understand the concept of single inheritance better in the second example.

```dart
//code 4.2
class Animal {
  String name = "Animal";
  Animal(){
    print("I am Animal class constructor.");
  }
  Animal.namedConstructor(){
    print("This is parent animal named constructor.");
  }
  void showName(){
    print(this.name);
    print("Hi from ${this.name}");
  }
```

```dart
  void eat(){
    print("Animals eat everything depending on what type it
    is.");
  }
}

class Cat extends Animal {
  //overriding parent constructor
  //although constructors are not inherited
  Cat() : super(){
    print("I am child cat class overriding super Animal class.");
  }
  Cat.namedCatConstructor() : super.namedConstructor(){
    print("The child cat named constructor overrides the parent
    animal named constructor.");
  }

  @override
  void showName(){
    print("Hi from cat.");
    print(this.name);
  }

  @override
  void eat(){
    super.eat();
    print("Cat doesn't eat vegetables..");
  }
}

class Cow extends Animal {
  //overriding parent constructor
  //although constructors are not inherited
```

```dart
  Cow() : super(){
    print("I am child cow class overriding super Animal
    class.");
  }
  Cow.namedCatConstructor() : super.namedConstructor(){
    print("The child cow named constructor overrides the parent
    animal named constructor.");
  }

  @override
  void showName(){
    print("Hi from cow.");
    print(this.name);
  }

  @override
  void eat(){
    super.eat();
    print("Cow does eat grass..");
  }
}

main(List<String> arguments){
  var cow = Cow();
  cow.name = "Daisy";
  cow.showName();
  var cat = Cat();
  cat.name = "Meaow";
  cat.showName();
  cat.eat();
  var anotherCat = Cat.namedCatConstructor();
}
```

We have added more lines in the parent class, created a new `Cow` class, and added some lines to both child classes; at the same time, we have added a few lines in our `main()` function to get the output.

Here is the new output:

```
//output of code 4.2
/home/ss/flutter/bin/cache/dart-sdk/bin/dart --enable-vm-
service:33101 /home/ss/IdeaProjects/bin/main.dart
Observatory listening on http://127.0.0.1:33101/

I am Animal class constructor.
I am child cow class overriding super Animal class.
Hi from cow.
Daisy
I am Animal class constructor.
I am child cat class overriding super Animal class.
Hi from cat.
Meaow
Animals eat everything depending on what type it is.
Cat doesn't eat vegetables..
This is parent animal named constructor.
The child cat named constructor overrides the parent animal
named constructor.

Process finished with exit code 0
```

You can see that more than one class can be based on a superclass.

Multilevel Inheritance

Let's consider the code first, and after looking at the output, we will discuss how multilevel inheritance works.

```dart
//code 4.3
class Animal {
  String name = "Animal";
  Animal(){
    print("I am Animal class constructor.");
  }
  Animal.namedConstructor(){
    print("This is parent animal named constructor.");
  }
  void showName(){
    print(this.name);
    print("Hi from ${this.name}");
  }
  void eat(){
    print("Animals eat everything depending on what type it
    is.");
  }
}

class Dog extends Animal {
  //overriding parent constructor
  //although constructors are not inherited
  Dog() : super(){
    print("I am child class dog overriding super Animal
    class.");
  }
```

```dart
  Dog.namedDogConstructor() : super.namedConstructor(){
    print("The child dog named constructor overrides the parent
    animal named constructor.");
  }
  Dog.anotherNamedConstructor(){
    print("This is parent Dog named constructor.");
  }
  @override
  void showName(){
    print("Hi from parent dog.");
    print(this.name);
  }
  @override
  void eat(){
    super.eat();
    print("Dog doesn't eat vegetables..");
  }
}

class PuppyDog extends Dog {
  //overriding parent constructor
  //although constructors are not inherited
  PuppyDog() : super(){
    print("I am child class puppy dog overriding my immediate
    parent Dog class.");
  }
  PuppyDog.namedDogConstructor() : super.anotherNamedConstructor(){
    print("The child puppy dog named constructor overrides the
    parent Dog another named constructor.");
  }
```

```dart
  @override
  void showName(){
    print("Hi from puppy dog.");
    print(this.name);
  }
  @override
  void eat(){
    super.eat();
    print("Puppy Dog eats milk only ...");
  }
}

main(List<String> arguments){
  var animal = Animal();
  animal.name = "Cow";
  animal.showName();
  var dog = Dog();
  dog.name = "Lucky";
  dog.showName();
  dog.eat();
  var anotherDog = Dog.namedDogConstructor();
  var puppy = PuppyDog();
  puppy.name = "I am offspring of Lucky";
  puppy.showName();
  puppy.eat();
  var anotherPuppy = PuppyDog.namedDogConstructor();
}
```

Here is the output:

```
//output of code 4.3
/home/ss/flutter/bin/cache/dart-sdk/bin/dart --enable-vm-
service:40767 /home/ss/IdeaProjects/bin/main.dart
Observatory listening on http://127.0.0.1:40767/
```

```
I am Animal class constructor.
Cow
Hi from Cow
I am Animal class constructor.
I am child class dog overriding super Animal class.
Hi from parent dog.
Lucky
Animals eat everything depending on what type it is.
Dog doesn't eat vegetables..
This is parent animal named constructor.
The child dog named constructor overrides the parent animal
named constructor.
I am Animal class constructor.
I am child class dog overriding super Animal class.
I am child class puppy dog overriding my immediate parent Dog class.
Hi from puppy dog.
I am offspring of Lucky
Animals eat everything depending on what type it is.
Dog doesn't eat vegetables..
Puppy Dog eats milk only ...
I am Animal class constructor.
This is parent Dog named constructor.
The child puppy dog named constructor overrides the parent Dog
another named constructor.

Process finished with exit code 0
```

In the previous code, the parent class is Animal. The Dog class inherits all its properties. After that, the Dog class has its offspring, a PuppyDog class. Now, the PuppyDog class inherits from the Dog class. Here, we have actually two child or base classes: Dog and PuppyDog. However, this is different from single inheritance because with multilevel inheritance, one child class is inherited from another child class.

In this example, the child class PuppyDog inherits from another child class, Dog. You can compare this tree of family lineage to a human's. I have a father, yet my father has a father, who is my grandfather, and on it goes.

Mixins: Adding More Features to a Class

Dart has a lot to offer when classes need to be reused; there is an important concept called a *mixin*. It is a way of reusing any class's code in multiple class hierarchies.

We can rewrite the previous code using mixins. All we need to do is use the keyword with. Suppose we have a class Dog that has a method canRun(). A Cat object can also run, can't it? Let's try the same code in a slightly different way.

```
//code 4.4
class Animal {
  String name = "Animal";
  Animal(){
    print("I am Animal class constructor.");
  }
  Animal.namedConstructor(){
    print("This is parent animal named constructor.");
  }
  void showName(){
    print(this.name);
  }
  void eat(){
    print("Animals eat everything depending on what type it
    is.");
  }
}
```

```
class Dog {
  void canRun(){
    print("I can run.");
  }
}

class Cat extends Animal with Dog {//reusing another class
  //overriding parent constructor
  //although constructors are not inherited
  Cat() : super(){
    print("I am child cat class overriding super Animal class.");
  }
  Cat.namedCatConstructor() : super.namedConstructor(){
    print("The child cat named constructor overrides the parent
    animal named constructor.");
  }
  @override
  void showName(){
    print("Hi from cat.");
  }
  @override
  void eat(){
    super.eat();
    print("Cat doesn't eat vegetables..");
  }
}

main(List<String> arguments){
  var cat = Cat();
  cat.name = "Meaow";
  cat.showName();
  cat.eat();
```

```
  var anotherCat = Cat.namedCatConstructor();
  anotherCat.canRun();
}
```

The subclass Cat has been extended, and at the same it has used mixins by reusing the Dog class's code. Look at this line:

```
class Cat extends Animal with Dog {...}
```

In the main() function, the Cat object uses the Dog class's method in this way:

```
anotherCat.canRun();
```

The output has not been changed except the last line, as shown here:

```
//output of code 4.4
I am Animal class constructor.
I am child cat class overriding super Animal class.
Hi from cat.
Animals eat everything depending on what type it is.
Cat doesn't eat vegetables..
This is parent animal named constructor.
The child cat named constructor overrides the parent animal
named constructor.
I can run.
```

Remember, for mixins, you need to use the with keyword followed by one or more mixin names.

Note   Support for mixins was introduced in Dart 2.1. Before that, in such cases, an abstract class was used. In the next chapter, you will learn about abstract classes and methods.

Mixins are a kind of limited multiple inheritance; in the previous code, we extend from one class (`Animal`) and then use a mixin to bring in features from another (`Dog`).

You should notice one characteristic here; at every stage, we use only classes. We can inherit from a class, and we can also use a class as a mixin using the `with` keyword.

In the next chapter, we'll add another feature: interfaces. These build a contract between two classes so we don't have to hard-code a class's functionality into another class. As long as a class conforms to the contract, we can change it without affecting the calling class.

CHAPTER 5

Entity Relationships: Abstract Classes, Interfaces, and Exception Handling

In the previous chapter, you learned that entities do not exist in isolation. You saw some examples of inheritance. You will see more in a minute, although in different forms.

There are a few more types of relationships between classes. A relationship between each class is always defined beforehand so that we don't have to use same code again and again. Like C#, PHP, Python, and Java, in Dart, the classes in a program can be related to each other. Identifying and establishing the relationships between them is an important aspect of object-oriented programming (OOP).

Therefore, the main objective of this chapter is to learn how we can identify relationships between classes, how we can define abstract classes and methods, and how we can use interfaces. We'll also look at exception handling because it's affected by entity relationships, and we use inheritance and interfaces as part of efficient error handling.

© Sanjib Sinha 2020
S. Sinha, *Quick Start Guide to Dart Programming*,
https://doi.org/10.1007/978-1-4842-5562-9_5

Identifying Relationships Between Entities

In general, our challenge is to create an application that is as close as possible to the real world. To do that, in a software application, we relate classes and objects to each other in such a manner that they remain loosely coupled. They act and react with other classes and objects. This dynamism makes them as close as possible to the real world.

In OOP, objects perform actions in response to messages from other objects, defining the receiving object's behavior.

There are similarities and differences among the entities, objects, and classes as a whole. Let's take a look at the following observations:

- A bus is a kind of an automobile.

- A car is a kind of an automobile.

- An engine is a part of an automobile.

- A wheel is a part of an automobile.

- A driver drives a car.

The preceding entities represent different objects and classes; still, they are related to each other. Furthermore, they should be loosely coupled; if one gets affected, that does not have any effect on the other (for example, if the design of a steering wheel on a car changes, the relationship with the driver does not). Now, based on the preceding observations, we can summarize our entity relationships in the following manner:

- Inheritance relationship

- Composition relationship

- Utilization relationship

- Instantiation relationship

In the previous chapter, you saw examples of inheritance. We can say that an automobile is a superclass of a car and bus. On the other hand, car and bus are subclasses. They derive features defined in the base class or superclass automobile. They have a relationship where one object is a type of another object, yet the reverse is not true. Every car is an automobile, but every automobile is not a car. Recall that Dart allows single inheritance and multilevel inheritance. Multiple inheritance in Dart is not allowed, although you can compensate that with the help of mixins, as we saw in Chapter 4.

Let's consider another set of relationships.

- A human is a kind of mammal.

- A cat is a kind of mammal.

- A tiger is a kind of cat.

- A lion is a kind of cat.

Now we can depict this relationship in Figure 5-1.

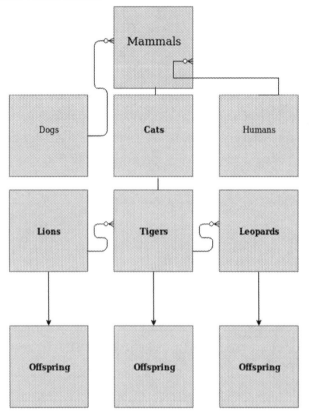

Figure 5-1. *A simple relationship between mammal entities*

In Figure 5-1, there is a set of classes: mammals, dogs, cats, humans, lions, tigers, leopards, and their offspring classes. The superclass mammals have the following set of characteristics:

- They are warm-blooded.

- They are vertebrates.

- They all have external ears.

- They all have internal brains covered by skulls.

We can say that dog, cat, and humans have similarities; they have
similar characteristics because they have inherited these attributes from
the superclass mammals. However, subclass cat is a superclass of lions,
tigers, and leopards; therefore, they will have similarities that they don't
share with dogs and humans.

One key feature of object-oriented programming in Dart is it allows us to
create an object that includes another object as its part. This mechanism of
creating an object is called *composition relationship*. Keeping Figure 5-1 in
mind, we can conclude that humans and tigers do not have a composition
relationship, whereas cats and tigers have a composition relationship. It is
called *composition* because one class has some traits in other classes that are
directly related to the previous class. Cat, Tiger, Lion, etc., are examples.

A utilization relationship is different. Consider Figure 5-1. A human
can use a dog to hunt, for example. Dart allows a class to make use of
another class.

An instantiation relationship is nothing but a relation between a class
and its object or instance. John is an object of a human class. When we
create a John object, we use the mammal class as an abstract superclass.

In the next section, you will see how we can use abstract classes.

Using Abstract Classes

An abstract class is used to provide a partial class implementation, leaving
the unimplemented piece to a subclass. Abstract methods can exist only in
abstract classes. In abstract methods, we just leave a semicolon (;) at the
end of the method name. We don't define the method body.

An abstract class is also where we can define an interface but leave its
implementation up to other classes. As I said at the end of Chapter 4, an
interface is a contract between two classes. Any class, abstract or concrete,
in Dart can be an interface. It's just much more common to use an abstract
class and leave the specifics up to the child class.

These are two key points to remember when you write an abstract class:

- You cannot create an instance of an abstract class.

- You cannot declare an abstract method outside an abstract class.

```
//code 5.1
//we cannot instantiate any abstract class
abstract class volume{
  //we can declare instance variable
  int age;
  void increase();
  void decrease();
  // a normal function
  void anyNormalFunction(int age){
    print("This is a normal function to know the $age.");
  }
}

class soundSystem extends volume{
  void increase(){
    print("Sound is up.");
  }
  void decrease(){
    print("Sound is down.");
  }
  //it is optional to override the normal function
  void anyNormalFunction(int age){
    print("This is a normal function to know how old the sound
    system is: $age.");
  }
}
```

```dart
main(List<String> arguments){
  var newSystem = soundSystem();
  newSystem.increase();
  newSystem.decrease();
  newSystem.anyNormalFunction(10);
}
```

Here is the output of the previous code:

```
Sound is up.
Sound is down.
This is a normal function to know how old the sound system is: 10.
```

We have used the `abstract` modifier to define an abstract class that cannot be instantiated.

So, we can say that the abstract class and methods summarize the main ideas, and we can extend that idea.

There are a few more things to remember about an abstract class in Dart.

- In an abstract class, we can also use normal properties and methods.

- It is optional to override the method.

- We can also define instance variables in the abstract class.

Consider the following code to understand how abstract classes in Dart are different from other object-oriented programming languages:

```dart
//code 5.2
abstract class Mammal {
  void run();
  void walk();
```

```
  void sound(){
    print("Mammals make sound");
  }
}

class Human implements Mammal {

  void run(){
    print("I am running.");
  }
  void walk(){
    print("I am walking");
  }
  void sound(){
    print("Humans make sound");
  }
}

main(List<String> arguments){
  var John = Human();
  print("John says: ");
  John.run();
  print("John says: ");
  John.walk();
  print("John makes no sound.");
  John.sound();
}
```

Here is the output where we can clearly see how we overrode the
abstract method:

```
//output of code 5.2
/home/ss/flutter/bin/cache/dart-sdk/bin/dart --enable-vm-
service:35727 /home/ss/IdeaProjects/bin/main.dart
Observatory listening on http://127.0.0.1:35727/
```

```
John says:
I am running.
John says:
I am walking
John makes sound.
Humans make sound

Process finished with exit code 0
```

Advantages of Interfaces

In some cases, we need to use reference variables and methods of many classes at the same time. Mixins can help. But there is another good feature in Dart: we can also use an interface.

An interface defines the syntactical contract that all the derived classes should follow. You will see in a minute how that works.

Let's see the code first, and then we will discuss it in detail. Remember that an interface in Dart is written as a class, but we don't extend; we implement it.

```
//code 5.3
// interface in Dart is a class, but we don't extend,
// we implement it
class Vehicle {
  void steerTheVehicle() {
    print("The vehicle is moving.");
  }
}

class Engine {
  //in the interface
  final _name; // final means single assignment and it must
               have an initializer as I use here
  //not in the interface, since it is a constructor
```

```
  Engine(this._name);
  String lessOilConsumption(){
    return "It consumes less oil.";
  }
}

class Car implements Vehicle, Engine{
  var _name;

  void steerTheVehicle() {
    print("The car is moving.");
  }

  String lessOilConsumption(){
    print("This model of car consumes less oil.");
  }

  void ridingExperience() => print("This car gives good ride,
  because it is an ${this._name}");
}

main(List<String> arguments){
  var car = Car();
  car._name = "Opel";
  print("Car name: ${car._name}");
  car.steerTheVehicle();
  car.lessOilConsumption();
  car.ridingExperience();
}
```

Here is the output of the previous code:

```
Car name: Opel
The car is moving.
This model of car consumes less oil.
This car gives good ride, because it is an Opel
```

When a class implements an interface, it implicitly defines all the
instance members of the implemented interface. A class implements one
or more interfaces at a time by declaring the implements keyword.

Considering the previous code, we see that class Car supports class
Vehicle and class Engine's API, and for that requirement, the class Car
implements class Vehicle and class Engine's interfaces. You can see the
Car object can call methods specified in Vehicle and Engine, as well as its
own methods.

An interface is used when we need a standard structure of methods; it
is not necessary that you should implement the interface members within
any interface. Consider this code:

```
//code 5.4
class OrderDetails {
  void UpdateCustomers(){
  }
  void TakeOrder(){
  }
}

class ItemDetails implements OrderDetails{
  void UpdateCustomers(){
    //implementing interface members
    print("Updating customers.");
  }
  void TakeOrder(){
    //implementing interface members
    print("Taking orders from customers.");
  }
}
```

```
main(List<String> arguments){
  var book = ItemDetails();
  book.TakeOrder();
  book.UpdateCustomers();
}
```

Now, look at the output, shown here:

```
//output of code 5.4
/home/ss/flutter/bin/cache/dart-sdk/bin/dart --enable-vm-
service:40359 /home/ss/IdeaProjects/bin/main.dart
Observatory listening on http://127.0.0.1:40359/

Taking orders from customers.
Updating customers.

Process finished with exit code 0
```

What happens if we don't follow this standard structure? When we implement an interface, we should implement interface members.

The next code snippet and the output will explain this:

```
//code 5.5
class OrderDetails {
  void UpdateCustomers(){
  }
  void TakeOrder(){
  }
}

class ItemDetails implements OrderDetails{
  void UpdateCustomers(){
    //implementing interface members
    print("Updating customers.");
  }
```

```
  /*
  void TakeOrder(){
    //implementing interface members
    print("Taking orders from customers.");
  }
  */
}

main(List<String> arguments){
  var book = ItemDetails();
  //book.TakeOrder();
  book.UpdateCustomers();
}
```

We didn't implement the interface member TakeOrder(). We have commented out that part of the preceding code.

In this case, the exceptions raised in Android Studio and the errors given as output tell us what we should have done. Look at the output:

```
//output of code 5.5
/home/ss/flutter/bin/cache/dart-sdk/bin/dart --enable-vm-
service:34271 /home/ss/IdeaProjects/bin/main.dart
Observatory listening on http://127.0.0.1:34271/

bin/main.dart:40:7: Error: The non-abstract class 'ItemDetails'
is missing implementations for these members:
 - OrderDetails.TakeOrder
Try to either
 - provide an implementation,
 - inherit an implementation from a superclass or mixin,
 - mark the class as abstract, or
 - provide a 'noSuchMethod' implementation.

class ItemDetails implements OrderDetails{
      ^^^^^^^^^^^
```

```
bin/main.dart:36:8: Context: 'OrderDetails.TakeOrder' is
defined here.
  void TakeOrder(){
       ^^^^^^^^^


Process finished with exit code 254
```

From the previous output, it is clear that Dart clearly notices that we have not implemented a method when we should have. If there is an implementation in an abstract class, we can use it when we extend that class.

Consider this code:

```
//code 5.6
class OrderDetails {
  //int age;
  /*
  void anyNormalFunction(int age){
    print("This is a normal function to know the $age.");
  }
  */
  void UpdateCustomers(){
  }
  void TakeOrder(){
  }
}

abstract class CustomerDetails {
  void Customers(){
    print("A list of customers.");
  }
}
class ItemDetails extends CustomerDetails implements
OrderDetails {
```

```
  void anyNormalFunction(int age){
    print("This is a normal function to know the age: $age.");
  }
  void UpdateCustomers(){
    //implementing interface members
    print("Updating customers.");
  }

  void TakeOrder(){
  }

}

main(List<String> arguments){
  var book = ItemDetails();
  //book.TakeOrder();
  book.UpdateCustomers();
  book.anyNormalFunction(12);
  book.Customers();
}
```

In the preceding code, we extended the abstract class, and at the same time, we implemented the interface. The output is here:

```
//output of code 5.6
/home/ss/flutter/bin/cache/dart-sdk/bin/dart --enable-vm-
service:39205 /home/ss/IdeaProjects/bin/main.dart
Observatory listening on http://127.0.0.1:39205/

Updating customers.
This is a normal function to know the age: 12.
A list of customers.

Process finished with exit code 0
```

You can see that the abstract class's `Customers()` method is called when we don't implement it ourselves.

There is another major difference between an abstract class and an interface. An abstract class can use normal properties and methods. However, it will give errors if we don't implement any part of an interface, in other words, if we leave the interface to keep its own implementation of a property or method. Look at this code and its output:

```
//code 5.7
class OrderDetails {
  int age;
  void anyNormalFunction(int age){
    print("This is a normal function to know the $age.");
  }

  void UpdateCustomers(){
  }
  void TakeOrder(){
  }
}

abstract class CustomerDetails {
  void Customers(){
  }
}

class ItemDetails extends CustomerDetails implements
OrderDetails {
//trying to implement interface normal functions
  void anyNormalFunction(int age){
    print("This is a normal function to know the age: $age.");
  }
```

```dart
  void UpdateCustomers(){
    //implementing interface members
    print("Updating customers.");
  }

  void TakeOrder(){
  }

  void Customers(){
  }

}

main(List<String> arguments){
  var book = ItemDetails();
  //book.TakeOrder();
  book.UpdateCustomers();
  book.anyNormalFunction(12);
}
```

Here is the error report:

```
//output of code 5.7
/home/ss/flutter/bin/cache/dart-sdk/bin/dart --enable-vm-
service:38747 /home/ss/IdeaProjects/bin/main.dart
Observatory listening on http://127.0.0.1:38747/

bin/main.dart:50:7: Error: The non-abstract class 'ItemDetails'
is missing implementations for these members:
 - OrderDetails.age
Try to either
 - provide an implementation,
 - inherit an implementation from a superclass or mixin,
 - mark the class as abstract, or
 - provide a 'noSuchMethod' implementation.
```

```
class ItemDetails extends CustomerDetails implements
OrderDetails {
      ^^^^^^^^^^^^
```
```
bin/main.dart:34:7: Context: 'OrderDetails.age' is defined here.
  int age;
      ^^^
```
```
Process finished with exit code 254
```

Therefore, here are a few things to remember about interfaces in Dart:

- The biggest advantage of interfaces is that we can implement multiple interfaces. Since multiple inheritance is not allowed in Dart, we can design our application in a way so that we can mimic inheriting multiple classes using interfaces. However, we cannot use any normal properties and behaviors in interfaces.

- Although we cannot inherit multiple classes through inheritance, we can overcome that limitation by combining abstract classes, interfaces, and mixins.

Static Variables and Methods

To implement class-wide variables and methods, we use the static keyword. Static variables are also called *class variables*. Let's first see a code snippet, and after that, we will discuss the advantages and disadvantages of static variables and methods.

```
//code 5.8
// static variables and methods consume less memory
// they are lazily initialized
class Circle{
  static const pi = 3.14;
```

```
static void drawACircle(){
  //from static method you cannot call a normal function
  print(pi);
}

void aNonStaticFunction(){
  //from a normal function or method you can call a static meethod
  Circle.drawACircle();
  print("This is normal function.");
}
}

main(List<String> arguments){
  var circle = Circle();
  circle.aNonStaticFunction();
  Circle.drawACircle();
}
```

Here is the output:

```
3.14
This is normal function.
3.14
```

As you see, static variables are useful for class-wide state and constants. So, in the main() method, we can add this line at the end:

```
main(List<String> arguments){
  var circle = Circle();
  circle.aNonStaticFunction();
  Circle.drawACircle();
  print(Circle.pi);
}
```

We get the value of constant `pi` again. Here, `Circle.pi` is the class variable, and the class method is `Circle.drawACircle()`. The biggest advantage of using static variables and methods is it consumes less memory. An instance variable, once instantiated, consumes memory whether it is being used or not. The static variables and methods are not initialized until they are used in the program. It consumes memory when they are used. By the way, it is also important to note that constants make maintenance easier and make programs easier to read.

Here are a few things to remember:

- From a normal function, you can call a static method.

- From a static method, you cannot call a normal function.

- In a static method, you cannot use the `this` keyword. This is because the static methods do not operate on an instance and thus do not have access to `this`.

So, in the end, we can conclude that using static variables and methods depends on the context and situations.

Exception Handling

During the execution of any program, some errors can occur that will disrupt the flow of the program automatically. These errors are called *exceptions*. In the exception handling cases, the class `Exception` is the superclass of all exceptions to prevent the application from terminating abruptly. This is why I'm covering exception handling in Chapter 7.

Figure 5-2 illustrates this concept where a computing process has two possible outputs. One could be the processed data we wanted, and another could be an error. We should enable ourselves to catch this error before it gives an ugly exception on the user's interface.

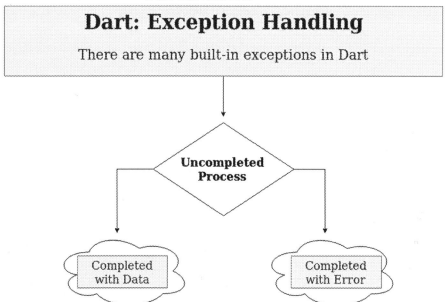

Figure 5-2. *Any uncompleted process could lead us to two possible
outputs*

Suppose you want to divide a number by zero. It is an impossible task
and will disrupt the flow, resulting in some errors. However, you cannot
control a user's behavior, so you need to take every precaution to handle
errors gracefully.

Dart programmers have thought about it, and they have included many
built-in exception classes. One of them is IntegerDivisionByZeroException;
it is thrown when a number is divided by zero. Likewise, when a
scheduled timeout happens while waiting for an asynchronous result,
the timeout exception occurs. If deferred libraries fail to load, there is
DeferredLoadException that happens.

Suppose a string cannot be parsed because it does not have the proper
format. In that case, FormatException occurs. Any input- and output-
related exceptions are captured through the IOException class.

Let's see some code snippets so that we can understand easily how we can catch the exceptions.

```
//code 5.9
main(List<String> arguments){
  try{
    int result = 10 ~/ 0;
    print("The result is $result");
  } on IntegerDivisionByZeroException{
    print("We cannot divide by zero");
  }
  try{
    int result = 10 ~/ 0;
    print("The result is $result");
  } catch(e){
    print(e);
  }
  try{
    int result = 10 ~/ 0;
    print("The result is $result");
  } catch(e){
    print("The exception is : $e");
  } finally{
    print("This is finally and it always is executed.");
  }
}
```

We have caught these errors before they give some ugly output to the user.

```
//the output of code 5.9
We cannot divide by zero
IntegerDivisionByZeroException
The exception is : IntegerDivisionByZeroException
This is finally and it always is executed.
```

As you can see in the output, there are several methods through which
we can catch the exceptions. If we know the type of exception, we can use
try/on, as we have used in the following previous code:

```
try{
  int result = 10 ~/ 0;
  print("The result is $result");
} on IntegerDivisionByZeroException{
  print("We cannot divide by zero");
}
```

In this case, we did know what type of exception can be generated.
So, we have used try/on. But what happens when we do not know the
exception?

In most cases, presumably a beginner will not know all the exception
classes that are predefined in Dart libraries. However, it is important to
know a few, which I have mentioned previously. Besides, the main reason
to wrap our code inside the try/catch block is this: we may have errors in
our code. Our code may contain problems. As a programmer, we should
not take any risks.

The syntax of handling exception is the following:

```
try{
  int result = 10 ~/ 0;
  print("The result is $result");
} catch(e){
  print(e);
}
```

The catch block is used when the handler needs the exception object.

The try block can be followed by the finally block after the catch block. We used the same thing in the following previous code:

```
try{
  int result = 10 ~/ 0;
  print("The result is $result");
} catch(e){
  print("The exception is : $e");
} finally{
  print("This is finally and it always is executed.");
}
```

The finally block will be executed at the end, whatever the outcome:

```
The exception is : IntegerDivisionByZeroException
This is finally and it always is executed.
```

If an exception occurs in the try block, the control goes to the catch block; and at the end, the finally block gives the output.

We can now wrap this section up with Figure 5-3 that depicts how many types of exception handling are used in Dart with the help of Exception classes.

In Figure 5-3, you will find the term *stack trace*. When a program is run, memory is allocated in two places, the stack and the heap. If there is a problem in our code, before allocating the memory, some events fire, and this can be traced in the stack. Simply put, a stack trace is the list of method calls that the application was in the middle of when an exception was thrown. We will look for the topmost method and know where the errors happen. In Dart, you will have to read the stack trace report; I am sure you will learn many things about how a program is run.

In addition, we can create our custom exception handling class that will catch the error. Why do we need that? You can add more flexibility to your code by building custom exception handling to give more useful names to exceptions, for example. However, I won't suggest as a beginner you should get your hands dirty with building custom exception classes immediately.

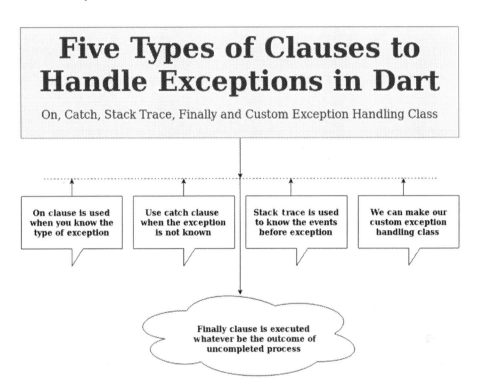

Figure 5-3. *Five types of exception handling in Dart*

We can also finally finish the task completely with a single codebase where we get through all the clauses of exception handling.

```
//code 5.10
class InputException implements Exception {
  String customException() {
    return "The input of negative number is not valid.";
  }
}
```

```dart
void main() {
  // ON Clause is used when the exception is known
  try {
    var res = 4 ~/ 0;
    print("The result: $res");
  } on IntegerDivisionByZeroException {
    print("You cannot divide by zero, the value is undefined");
  }

  // CATCH Clause is used when exception is unknown
  try {
    var res = 3 ~/ 0;
    print("The result is $res");
  } catch (e) {
    print("The exception thrown is $e");
  }

  // STACK TRACE is used to know the steps of the events
  // these events took place before the actual Exception was
  //   thrown
  try {
    int res = 10 ~/ 0;
    print("The result is $res");
  } catch (e, s) {
    print("The exception: $e");
    print("Stack trace is \n $s");
  }

  // FINALLY Clause is always Executed
  // whether exception is thrown or not
  try {
    int res = 9 ~/ 0;
    print("The result: $res");
```

```
  } catch (e) {
    print("The exception: $e");
  } finally {
    print("The finally clause is always executed.");
  }

  // we can make our Custom Exception by creating a class
  try {
    inputValue(-14);
  } catch (e) {
    print(e.customException());
  } finally {
    print("The finally clause is always executed");
  }
}

void inputValue(int inputNumber) {
  if (inputNumber < 0) {
    var inputException = InputException();
    throw inputException;
  }
}
```

Note the use of the throw keyword in the inputValue() function. This throws the specified exception and passes control back to the calling code. The try/catch block can then handle this thrown exception. Now we can take a look at the output to see the stack trace:

```
//output of code 5.10
/home/ss/Downloads/flutter/bin/cache/dart-sdk/bin/dart
--enable-asserts --enable-vm-service:42201 /home/ss/
IdeaProjects/my_app/main.dart
Observatory listening on http://127.0.0.1:42201/eUtYODGP6ro=/
```

```
You cannot divide by zero, the value is undefined
The exception thrown is IntegerDivisionByZeroException
The exception: IntegerDivisionByZeroException
Stack trace is
#0      int.~/ (dart:core-patch/integers.dart:18:7)
#1      main (file:///home/ss/IdeaProjects/my_app/main.
        dart:24:18)
#2      _startIsolate.<anonymous closure> (dart:isolate-patch/
        isolate_patch.dart:301:19)
#3      _RawReceivePortImpl._handleMessage (dart:isolate-patch/
        isolate_patch.dart:172:12)

The exception: IntegerDivisionByZeroException
The finally clause is always executed.
The input of negative number is not valid.
The finally clause is always executed

Process finished with exit code 0
```

Now, it entirely depends on the developer how they handle the exception. All we should remember is that the user will not like it if an exception is raised by the code. Therefore, it is mandatory to go through the test before going live, and it is always better to use an exception handling mechanism where needed.

CHAPTER 6

Anonymous Functions

In Dart, most of the functions we have seen so far are named functions, which are similar to functions in languages like C# and Java. Still, the function syntax of Dart has more similarities with JavaScript than in many strongly typed languages like C# or Java.

Because in Dart everything is object, a function is also an object; this means we can store it in a variable and use it anywhere in our application. The advantage of Dart is we that can pass a function like any other type, such as string, integer, etc. These features are greatly enhanced when the functions have no names at all. These nameless functions act the same as named functions; they can have any number of parameters, including zero parameters. The type annotations are optional.

These functions are called *anonymous functions*. Like named functions, we can assign any anonymous function to a function object variable. We can also pass it to another function.

Lambdas, higher-order functions, and lexical closures all are anonymous functions, and they have some similarities. In their namelessness and anonymity, these features of Dart are very interesting. Let's start with lambdas. Then we will discuss higher-order functions and closures. In reality, you will find that lambdas actually implement higher-order functions.

© Sanjib Sinha 2020
S. Sinha, *Quick Start Guide to Dart Programming*,
https://doi.org/10.1007/978-1-4842-5562-9_6

A First Look at Lambdas

Figure 6-1 shows how we can use lambdas, one type of anonymous function.

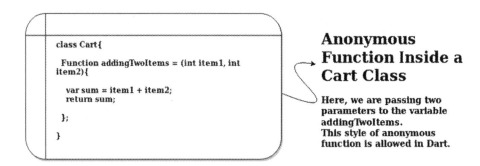

```
class Cart{

  Function addingTwoItems = (int item1, int
item2){

    var sum = item1 + item2;
    return sum;

  };

}
```

Anonymous Function Inside a Cart Class

Here, we are passing two parameters to the variable addingTwoItems.
This style of anonymous function is allowed in Dart.

In the above Figure, An anonymous function is defined and assigned to a variable named addingTwoItems. The ; is used to terminate the variable assignment.

Figure 6-1. *An anonymous function is assigned to a variable*

In Figure 6-1, the longhand version of the anonymous function needs a terminating semicolon; this is because we assign the value to a variable named addingTwoItems. In addition, the longhand version, we can use the fat arrow notation, as covered in Chapter 5. Figure 6-2 shows the two types of anonymous functions and how we can use them in our application. We will also see the code in a minute.

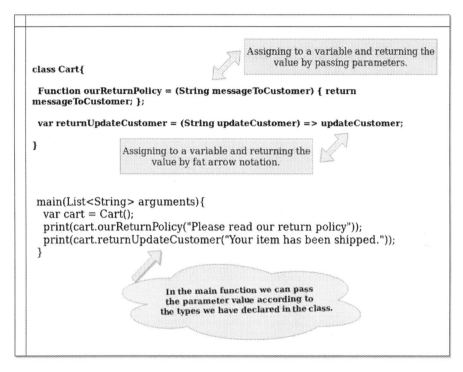

Figure 6-2. *Two types of declaring anonymous functions*

In Figure 6-2, we mentioned the type of parameters. In case we didn't mention it, Dart dynamically allocates them.

Let's look at the code of Figure 6-1 and see the output also to understand this concept.

```
//code 6.1
class Cart{

  Function addingTwoItems = (int item1, int item2){

    var sum = item1 + item2;
    return sum;

  };

}
```

```
main(List<String> arguments){

  var cart = Cart();
  print("Your total price is:");
  print(cart.addingTwoItems(120, 458));
}
```

Here is the output of this code:

```
//output of code 6.1
Your total price is:
578
```

The code used in Figure 6-2 is shown next. We used two methods to declare anonymous functions: longhand and shorthand.

```
//code 6.2
class Cart{

  Function ourReturnPolicy = (String messageToCustomer) {
    return messageToCustomer;
};

  var returnUpdateCustomer = (String updateCustomer) =>
  updateCustomer;

}

main(List<String> arguments){
  var cart = Cart();
  print(cart.ourReturnPolicy("Please read our return policy"));
  print(cart.returnUpdateCustomer("Your item has been
  shipped."));
}
```

The output is quite straightforward. We passed one parameter with each function and get this string output:

```
//output of code 6.2
Please read our return policy
Your item has been shipped.
```

Here we summarize the key features of anonymous functions:

- We can declare any anonymous function without a function name.

- We can assign it to a variable.

- The anonymous function can be passed into another function, as we'll see later.

- In the longhand version, we need to use a semicolon to terminate the statement because we assign it to a variable.

- The only disadvantage of an anonymous function is we cannot use it recursively as it has no name.

Exploring Higher-Order Functions

The specialty of higher-order functions is that they can accept a function as a parameter. That is why they are called higher-order functions. They not only can accept a function as a parameter; they can also return it.

Let's look at the following simple code snippet to get accustomed to the idea:

```
//code 6.3
//returning a function
Function DividingByFour(){
  Function LetUsDivide = (int x) => x ~/ 4;
  return LetUsDivide;
}
```

```
main(List<String> arguments){
  var result = DividingByFour();
  print(result(56));
}
```

The output is 14.

So, we return the LetUsDivide() function quite easily through a higher-order function called Function DividingByFour().

Let's see some more examples to understand how anonymous functions work. Look at this line in the previous code:

```
Function LetUsDivide = (int x) => x ~/ 4;
```

The function LetUsDivide() is assigned to an anonymous function called (int x). Then we used fat arrow notation to return a value.

The main advantage is that we can store functions in a variable or reference them by the name of the variable. Having a variable containing a function object gives us freedom to pass it around the application like any other variable. Furthermore, we can return a function object stored in a variable, or we can pass it into another function where we can call it as any declared function.

In the next section, we will see how the concept of closures changes according to the situation.

A Closure Is a Special Function

We can define closure in two ways.

- We can say that a closure is the only function that has access to the parent scope, even after the scope is closed.

- The term *closure* is derived from the term *close-over*. Since it wraps any nonlocal variable that was valid at the time of declaration, it actually closes over that variable.

When one function is returned by another function, we can say that closures are *formed*; the same thing happens in higher-order functions.

The next example will explain this concept. To understand this definition, let's look at the following short code snippet where an anonymous function closure is overriding the parent scope:

```
//code 6.4
//a closure can modify the parent scope
String message = "Any Parent String";
Function overridingParentScope = (){
  String message = "Overriding the parent scope";
  print(message);
};

main(List<String> arguments){
  print(message);
  overridingParentScope();
}
```

The output is as follows:

```
Any Parent String
Overriding the parent scope
```

In the second definition, we can say that a closure is a function object that has access to the variables in its lexical scope, even when the function is used outside of its original scope.

```
//code 6.5
//declaring an anonymous function without any parameter
Function show = (){
  Function gettingImage(){
    String path = "This is a new path to image.";
```

```
    print(path);
  }
  return gettingImage;
};

main(List<String> arguments){
  String path = "This is an old path.";
  var showing = show();
  showing();
}
```

Here is the output:

```
This is a new path to image.
```

This code actually returns a function object called gettingImage that has accessed the variable in its lexical scope. Dart is a lexically scoped language that means the innermost scope is searched first.

So, at the end of this section, we can summarize a few points about closures.

- In several other languages, including Python and PHP, you are not allowed to modify the parent variable.

- However, within a closure, you can mutate or modify the values of variables present in the parent scope.

Figure 6-3 shows a little more detail about closures (specifically their underlying types when they are created).

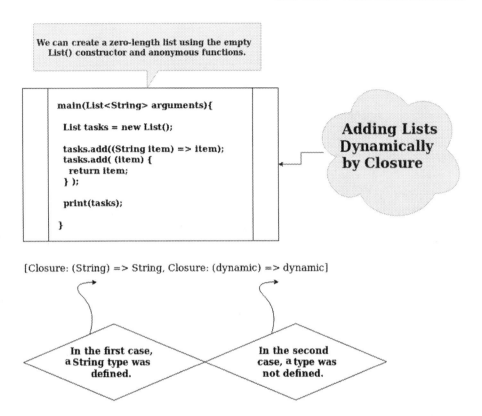

Figure 6-3. *In the output, Dart recognizes this anonymous function as a closure*

Bringing It All Together

Now we will conclude our journey of studying the nameless or anonymous functions in a single codebase, and we will also look at the output. In the following code snippet, we have tried to give you a feel of all the types of anonymous functions. Read the comments in the code to see what types of anonymous functions we are using here.

```
//code 6.6
//Lambda is an anonymous function
class AboutLambdas{
  //first way of expressing Lambda or anonymous function
  Function addingNumbers = (int a, int b){
    var sum = a + b;

    return sum;
  };
  Function multiplyWithEight = (int num){
    return num * 8;
  };

  //second way of expressing Lambda by Fat Arrow
  Function showName = (String name) => name;

  //higher order functions pass function as parameter
  int higherOrderFunction(Function myFunction){
    int a = 10;
    int b = 20;
    print(myFunction(a, b));
  }

  //returning a function
  Function returningAFunction(){
    Function showAge = (int age) => age;
    return showAge;
  }

  //a closure can modify the parent scope
  String anyString = "Any Parent String";
  Function overridingParentScope = (){
    String message = "Overriding the parent scope";
    print(message);
  };
```

```
Function show = (){
  // the anonymous function will return this originally
  Function gettingImage(){ // anonymous function returns a
                             function
    String path = "This is a new path to image.";
    print(path);
  }
  return gettingImage;
};
}

main(List<String> arguments){
  var add = AboutLambdas();
  var addition = add.addingNumbers(5, 10);
  print(addition);
  var mul = AboutLambdas();
  var result = mul.multiplyWithEight(4);
  print(result);
  var name = AboutLambdas();
  var myName = name.showName("Sanjib");
  print(myName);
  var higher = AboutLambdas();
  var higherOrder = higher.higherOrderFunction(add.addingNumbers);
  higherOrder;
  var showAge = AboutLambdas();
  var showingAge = showAge.returningAFunction();
  print(showingAge(25));
  var sayMessage = AboutLambdas();
  sayMessage.overridingParentScope();
  var image = AboutLambdas();
  String path = "This is an old path.";
```

```
  var imagePath = image.show();
  imagePath();
}
```

The output shows how the nameless functions work.

```
//output of code 8.6
15
32
Sanjib
30
25
Overriding the parent scope

This is a new path to image.
```

CHAPTER 7

Data Structures and Collections

Understanding the concepts of data structures and collections, as a whole, plays a crucial role in your future Dart programming. You will learn in a minute that there are four types of data structures in Dart.

- List
- Set
- Map
- Queue

In my opinion, Lists and Maps will cover almost everything, so you hardly need the other two types in your programming life, except on a few occasions. However, my suggestion is to not ignore learning about Set and Queue; on a few occasions, they have incalculable worth. We will discuss them in this chapter in detail.

Figure 7-1 shows what type of collections we are going to use.

© Sanjib Sinha 2020
S. Sinha, *Quick Start Guide to Dart Programming*,
https://doi.org/10.1007/978-1-4842-5562-9_7

Core Interfaces of Collections in Dart

There are four types of data structure of which Lists and Maps are mostly used in building applications.

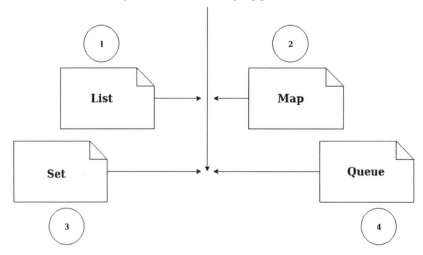

Figure 7-1. *All types of collections in Dart*

You will learn about these data structures in this chapter. We will cover all the concepts of Dart collections in detail. Moving/processing collections of data in a type-safe manner is always our priority in software development. To do that, first we need to have a basic understanding of how to organize a large chunk of data for later retrieval.

In a nutshell, data structures help you to organize information for storage and later retrieval.

Using the built-in collection classes in Dart is a big advantage to us. List and Map both fall into this category. They allow us to manipulate lists of data, and they allow us to access the collections of data in a type-safe manner; furthermore, we can benefit from the additional validations done by the type checker provided by Dart. Not only that, the built-in utilities provided by Dart help us to access elements directly in Lists and Maps; you will also learn how to build Maps and Lists from preexisting values.

So, let's start with Lists.

Lists: An Ordered Collection

A list is a simple ordered group of objects. Creating a List seems easy because the Dart core libraries have the necessary support and a `List` class. There are two types of Lists.

- Fixed-length list

- Growable list

In a fixed-length list, the length of the list cannot change at runtime; however, in the second type, a growable list, the length can change at runtime.

Figure 7-2 describes how these Lists works.

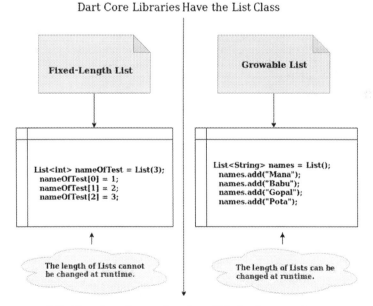

Figure 7-2. *Two types of Lists are available in Dart*

In the next examples, we will look at the two types of List separately. We will also see how they work. First simply create a List, as shown here:

```
void main() {
    var lst = new List();
    lst.add(3);
    lst.add(4);
    print(lst);
}
```

```
//output
[3, 4]
```

Now here's our first example:

```
//code 7.1
int listFunction(){
  List<int> nameOfTest = List(3);
  nameOfTest[0] = 1;
  nameOfTest[1] = 2;
  nameOfTest[2] = 3;

  //there are three methods to capture the list
  //1. method
  for(int element in nameOfTest){
    print(element);
  }
  print("-----------");

  //2. method
  nameOfTest.forEach((v) => print('${v}'));
  print("-----------");
```

```
  //3. method
  for(int i = 0; i < nameOfTest.length; i++){
    print(nameOfTest[i]);
  }
}

main(List<String> arguments){
  listFunction();
}
```

As you can see, this is an ordered list of three numbers. We are getting the output by using three methods, each of which is straightforward.

```
//output of code 7.1
1
2
3
-----------
1
2
3
-----------
1
2
3
```

The next example is of a growable list, shown here:

```
//code 7.2
Function growableList(){
  //1. method
  List<String> names = List();
  names.add("Mana");
  names.add("Babu");
```

```
    names.add("Gopal");
    names.add("Pota");

    //there are two methods to capture the list
    print("-----------");

    //1. method
    names.forEach((v) => print('${v}'));
    print("-----------");

    //2. method
    for(int i = 0; i < names.length; i++){
      print(names[i]);
    }
}

main(List<String> arguments){
  growableList();
}
```

This is also straightforward; we have not passed any number through List(), which lets us add any number of elements to it. Here we have added a few names. And we can capture the List elements through two methods, instead of three.

The output is quite expected, as shown here:

```
//output of code 7.2
-----------
Mana
Babu
Gopal
Pota
```

```
----------
Mana
Babu
Gopal
Pota
```

So, it is evident from the output and the code that growable lists are dynamic in nature. We can dynamically add any number of elements, and we can also remove elements it by a simple method: names.remove("any name"). We can also use the key; note that this ordered list starts from 0. So, we can remove the first name just by passing this key value: names. removeAt(0). We use the removeAt(key) method for that operation. We can also clear the Lists just by typing names.clear().

Consider another code listing, where we have used many default methods of the List class.

```
//code 7.3
main(){
  var number1 = 1;
  var number2 = 1;
  while(number2 < 50){
    print(number2);
    number2 += number1;
    number1 = number2 - number1;
  }
  print("Separator line: =============");
  var fibonacciNumbers = [1, 2, 3, 5, 8, 13, 21, 34];
  print(fibonacciNumbers.take(3).toList());
  print("Separator line: =============");
  print(fibonacciNumbers.skip(5).toList());
  print("Separator line: =============");
  print(fibonacciNumbers.skip(2).contains(5));
  print("Separator line: =============");
```

```
print(fibonacciNumbers.take(3).skip(2).take(1).toList());
print("Separator line: =============");
var clonedFibonacciNumbers = List.from(fibonacciNumbers);
print("Cloned list: $clonedFibonacciNumbers");
}
```

First, let's check the output.

```
//output of code 7.3
/home/ss/Downloads/flutter/bin/cache/dart-sdk/bin/dart
--enable-asserts --enable-vm-service:33845 /home/ss/
IdeaProjects/my_app/main.dart
Observatory listening on http://127.0.0.1:33845/6uljPm-VaFM=/

1
2
3
5
8
13
21
34
Separator line: =============
[1, 2, 3]
Separator line: =============
[13, 21, 34]
Separator line: =============
true
Separator line: =============
[3]
Separator line: =============
Cloned list: [1, 2, 3, 5, 8, 13, 21, 34]

Process finished with exit code 0
```

The separator line used in between the output helps show how the other default methods of the List class work.

We have used several default methods such as toList(), contains(), skip(), etc.

We can take any number of elements from the List class. We can eliminate the first two numbers and print other values.

There are also other List methods that are extremely flexible to add some special keywords to a List. Consider this small example first:

```
//code 7.4
main(){
  var names = ["John", "Robert", "Smith", "Peter"];
  names.forEach((name) => print(name));
}
```

It will give us some nice output of names.

```
//output of code 7.4
John
Robert
Smith
Peter
```

Can we add some extra functionality into this List of names so that they might have something in common? Suppose every name we have listed is absconding. We need to prepend each name with Absconding. The map() function gives us an opportunity to produce a new List by transforming each element at one go. Now the preceding code changes to this:

```
//code 7.5
main(){
  var names = ["John", "Robert", "Smith", "Peter"];
  names.forEach((name) => print(name));
```

```
  var mappedNames = names.map((name) => "Absconding $name").
  toList();
  print(mappedNames);
}
```

The output changes to this:

```
//output of code 7.5
John
Robert
Smith
Peter
[Absconding John, Absconding Robert, Absconding Smith,
Absconding Peter]
```

We have successfully mapped each element and transformed it, putting the results in a new list.

For further reading about the List class, you can go to the Dart language repositories on Lists:

```
https://api.dartlang.org/dev/2.0.0-dev.65.0/dart-core/List-
class.html
```

Set: An Unordered Collections of Unique Items

The heading says everything. A Set represents a collection of objects in which each object can occur only once. In the Dart core library, there is a Set class with this functionality.

Since Set is an unordered collection of unique items, you cannot get elements by index. There is a concept called a HashSet that actually implements the unordered Set, and it is based on a hashtable-based Set implementation. We will look into those features in a minute.

We can create sets in two ways.

```
Set <type> set name = {};
var setname = <Type> {};

//code 7.6
void setFunction(){
  //set is an unordered collections of unique items
  //cannot get elements by INDEX since the items are unordered
  //1. method of creating Set
  Set<String> countries = Set.from(['India', 'England', 'US']);
  Set<int> numbers = Set.from([1, 45, 58]);
  Set<int> moreNumbers = Set();
  moreNumbers.add(178);
  moreNumbers.add(568);
  moreNumbers.add(569);

  //1. method
  for(int element in numbers){
    print(element);
  }
  print("-----------");

  //2. method
  countries.forEach((v) => print('${v}'));

  print("-----------");
  for(int element in moreNumbers){
    if(moreNumbers.lookup(element) == 178){
      print(element);
      break;
    }
  }
}
```

```
  //set
  var fruitCollection = {'Mango', 'Apple', 'Jack fruit'};
  print(fruitCollection.lookup('Something Else'));
  //it gives null
  //lists
  List fruitCollections = ['Mango', 'Apple', 'Jack fruit'];
  var myIntegers = [1, 2, 3, 'non-integer object'];
  print(myIntegers[3]);
  print(fruitCollections[0]);
}

main(List<String> arguments){
  setFunction();
}
```

Let's look at the output first; then we will be able to understand what happens.

```
//output of code 7.6
1
45
58
-----------
India
England
US
-----------
178
null
non-integer object
Mango
```

We have created a Set of countries, numbers, and morenumbers; finally, we created a List at the end to distinguish between the characters of Lists and Sets.

These three methods have created Sets:

```
Set<String> countries = Set.from(['India', 'England', 'US']);
Set<int> numbers = Set.from([1, 45, 58]);
Set<int> moreNumbers = Set();
```

We get the output of the first one we have using this method:

```
countries.forEach((v) => print('${v}'));
```

The second List has been retrieved by this method:

```
for(int element in numbers){
  print(element);
}
```

We have captured the values of the third Set using this method:

```
for(int element in moreNumbers){
    if(moreNumbers.lookup(element) == 178){
      print(moreNumbers);
      break;
    }
 }
```

We used the lookup() method with each element of the List as the argument. When we match 178, we print the whole list.

To manipulate a Set, there are lots of methods available in the Dart core libraries. You can use moreNumbers.contains(value), moreNumbers. remove(value), moreNumbers.isEmpty(), etc.

In the following code snippet, the return value of lookup() is null, since there is no such value present in the Set:

```
//set
  var fruitCollection = {'Mango', 'Apple', 'Jack fruit'};
  print(fruitCollection.lookup('Something Else'));
```

We need to remember one thing. When the Set type is an integer, it is easier to use a for loop to loop over the elements. Otherwise, it is wise to use foreach as we have used in the previous code.

```
countries.forEach((v) => print('${v}'));
```

In the next section, we will see how Map in Dart works.

Maps: The Key-Value Pair

An unordered collection of key-value pairs is known as a Map in Dart. The main advantage of a Map is that the key-value pair can be of any type. The flexibility of extending and shrinking these unordered collections is another great advantage when managing a big chunk of data.

Figure 7-3 summarizes how Maps in Dart work.

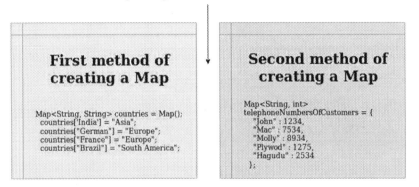

Figure 7-3. *Key-value pair of unordered collections in Dart*

To begin with, let's start with a few key features of Map that we should remember while we work with Map.

- Each key in a Map should be unique.

- The value can be repeated.

- The Map can commonly be called a hash or a dictionary.

- The size of a Map is not fixed; it can either increase or decrease as per the number of elements. In other words, Maps can grow or shrink at runtime.

- A HashMap is an implementation of a Map, and it is based on a hashtable.

Let's look at the following code snippet to understand how a Map works in Dart:

```
//code 7.7
void mapFunction(){
  //unordered collection of key=>value pair
  Map<String, String> countries = Map();
  countries['India'] = "Asia";
  countries["Germany"] = "Europe";
  countries["France"] = "Europe";
  countries["Brazil"] = "South America";

  //1. method we can obtain key or value
  for(var key in countries.keys){
    print("Country's name: $key");
  }
  print("-----------");
  for(String value in countries.values){
    print("Continent's name: $value");
  }

  //2. method
  countries.forEach((key, value) => print("Country: $key and
  Continent: $value"));
  //we can update any map very easily
  if(countries.containsKey("Germany")){
    countries.update("Germany", (value) => "European Union");
    print("Updated country Germany.");
    countries.forEach((key, value) => print("Country: $key and
    Continent: $value"));
  }
```

```
//we can remove any country
countries.remove("Brazil");
countries.forEach((key, value) => print("Country: $key and
Continent: $value"));
print("Barzil has been removed successfully.");
print("-----------");

//3. method of creating a map
Map<String, int> telephoneNumbersOfCustomers = {
   "John" : 1234,
   "Mac" : 7534,
   "Molly" : 8934,
   "Plywod" : 1275,
   "Hagudu" : 2534
};

telephoneNumbersOfCustomers.forEach((key, value) =>
print("Customer: $key and Contact Number: $value"));
}

main(List<String> arguments){
  mapFunction();
}
```

Here is the output of the previous code:

```
Country's name: India
Country's name: Germany
Country's name: France
Country's name: Brazil
-----------
Continent's name: Asia
Continent's name: Europe
Continent's name: Europe
```

```
Continent's name: South America
Country: India and Continent: Asia
Country: Germany and Continent: Europe
Country: France and Continent: Europe
Country: Brazil and Continent: South America
Updated country Germany.
Country: India and Continent: Asia
Country: Germany and Continent: European Union
Country: France and Continent: Europe
Country: Brazil and Continent: South America
Country: India and Continent: Asia
Country: Germany and Continent: European Union
Country: France and Continent: Europe
Barzil has been removed successfully.
-----------
Customer: John and Contact NUmber: 1234
Customer: Mac and Contact NUmber: 7534
Customer: Molly and Contact NUmber: 8934
Customer: Plywod and Contact NUmber: 1275
Customer: Hagudu and Contact NUmber: 2534
```

There are three methods that we can use to retrieve the values of a Map.

```
//1. method we can obtain key or value
for(var key in countries.keys){
 print("Country's name: $key");
}
print("-----------");

//2. Method
for(String value in countries.values){
 print("Continent's name: $value");
}
```

```
//3. method
countries.forEach((key, value) => print("Country: $key and
Continent: $value"));
```

In addition, there are several methods to add, update, or remove the elements in a Map.

Using Collections Together

We can combine Lists and Maps and test the validations. There is a lot of flexibility involved in Dart when we want to confirm that each element passes a particular test. Suppose we want to check that every user's age is over 18.

```
//code 7.8
main(){
  var name;
  var age;
  List<Map<String, dynamic>> users = [
    { name: "Peter", age: 18 },
    { name: "Mira", age: 20 },
    { name: "Jason", age: 22 },
  ];
  var is18AndOver = users.every((user) => user[age] >= 18);
  print(is18AndOver);

}
```

The output will be true. All users in our combined Lists and Maps are either 18 or older. We can also check whether every user's name starts with *A* or not. We use the same every() method in a different way. The following code snippet is interesting because here we have used an anonymous function:

```
//code 7.9
main(){
  var name;
  var age;
  List<Map<String, dynamic>> users = [
    { name: "Peter", age: 18 },
    { name: "Mira", age: 20 },
    { name: "Jason", age: 22 },
  ];
  var isEighteenAndOver = users.every((user) => user[age] >= 18);
  print(isEighteenAndOver);

  var hasNamesWithLetterA = users.every((user) => user.
  toString().startsWith("A"));
  print(hasNamesWithLetterA);

}
```

Let's look at the output in the editor's console this time:

```
//output of code 7.9
/home/ss/Downloads/flutter/bin/cache/dart-sdk/bin/dart
--enable-asserts --enable-vm-service:45239 /home/ss/
IdeaProjects/my_app/main.dart
Observatory listening on http://127.0.0.1:45239/o1AwiUzW7MQ=/

true
false

Process finished with exit code 0
```

The first test passes; however, the second test fails because every user's name does not start with the letter *A*.

Let's make this code more interesting with more options for testing. This time we have added more names to this list, mapping their age records to find how many users are older than 21.

```dart
//code 7.10
main(){
  var name;
  var age;
  List<Map<String, dynamic>> users = [
    { name: "Peter", age: 18 },
    { name: "Mira", age: 20 },
    { name: "Jason", age: 22 },
    { name: "Morgan", age: 32 },
    { name: "Mary", age: 50 },
    { name: "Will", age: 86 },
    { name: "Bruce", age: 96 },
  ];
  var isEighteenAndOver = users.every((user) => user[age] >= 18);
  print(isEighteenAndOver);

  var hasNamesWithLetterA = users.every((user) => user.
  toString().startsWith("A"));
  print(hasNamesWithLetterA);

  var overTwentyOne = users.where((user) => user[age] > 21);
  print(overTwentyOne.length);

}
```

Look at the output this time:

```
//output of code 7.10
true
false
5
```

There are five users altogether who have their ages older than 21. Next, we can make this test complete with the method singleWhere() to confirm that there are no users whose age is younger than 18.

```
//code 7.11
main(){
  var name;
  var age;
  List<Map<String, dynamic>> users = [
    { name: "Peter", age: 18 },
    { name: "Mira", age: 20 },
    { name: "Jason", age: 22 },
    { name: "Morgan", age: 32 },
    { name: "Mary", age: 50 },
    { name: "Will", age: 86 },
    { name: "Bruce", age: 96 },
  ];
  var isEighteenAndOver = users.every((user) => user[age] >= 18);
  print(isEighteenAndOver);

  var hasNamesWithLetterA = users.every((user) => user.
  toString().startsWith("A"));
  print(hasNamesWithLetterA);

  var overTwentyOne = users.where((user) => user[age] > 21);
  print(overTwentyOne.length);
```

```
  var underEighteen = users.singleWhere((user) => user[age]
  < 18, orElse: () => null);
  print(underEighteen);

}
```

Let's first see the output in our console, as shown here:

```
//output of code 7.11
/home/ss/Downloads/flutter/bin/cache/dart-sdk/bin/dart
--enable-asserts --enable-vm-service:36063 /home/ss/
IdeaProjects/my_app/main.dart
Observatory listening on http://127.0.0.1:36063/vr1OkScPAEw=/

true
false
5
null

Process finished with exit code 0
```

The last line of output tells us that there is no user who has an age younger than 18. We want you to look at the last bit of code here:

```
var underEighteen = users.singleWhere((user) => user[age] < 18,
orElse: () => null);
  print(underEighteen);
```

In the orElse conditional, we have used the anonymous function ()
=> null; this anonymous function returns null only when the condition is true.

Lastly, we will see another collection feature in Dart, which is called a Queue.

Queue Is Open-Ended

The queue is useful when you try to build a collection that can be added from one end and can be deleted from another end. The values are removed or read using an index based on the order of their insertion.

Consider this code:

```
//code 7.12
import 'dart:collection';   // we are about to import some extra
                            methods from collection library
main(List<String> arguments){
  Queue myQueue = new Queue();
  print("Default implementation ${myQueue.runtimeType}");

  myQueue.add("Sanjib");
  myQueue.add(54);
  myQueue.add("Howrah");
  myQueue.add("sanjib12sinha@gmail.com");
  for(var allTheValues in myQueue){
    print(allTheValues);
  }
  print("----------");

  print("We are removing the first element ${myQueue.
  elementAt(0)}.");
  myQueue.removeFirst();
  for(var allTheValues in myQueue){
    print(allTheValues);
  }
  print("----------");

  print("We are removing the last element ${myQueue.
  elementAt(2  )}.");
  myQueue.removeLast();
```

```
  for(var allTheValues in myQueue){
    print(allTheValues);
  }
}
```

The output gives us the full lists of what we have added in the Queue. After that, we have removed the first and last elements.

```
//output of code 7.12
Default implementation ListQueue<dynamic>
Sanjib
54
Howrah
sanjib12sinha@gmail.com
----------
We are removing the first element Sanjib.
54
Howrah
sanjib12sinha@gmail.com
----------
We are removing the last element sanjib12sinha@gmail.com.
54
Howrah
```

In most cases, as I said at the beginning of the chapter, we can handle this with Lists and Maps. So, Queue is an option that you may need sometimes, but not very often.

CHAPTER 8

Multithreaded Programming Using Future and Callable Classes

As you know, everything is an object in Dart. A class is an object. A function is also an object. Because of this object-oriented approach, objects should contain some methods to allow them to behave like functions. In this chapter, you will see how we can make them behave like functions. We will allow an instance of any class to behave like a function. Now Dart allows objects with call methods to be called and, at the same time, to be assigned to variables of a function type. In this chapter, we will look into one of the most important aspects of Dart programming, multithreaded programming using future and callable classes.

Callable Classes

Internally, Dart implicitly changes the `call()` method (like, `someVariable.call()`) to a closure. When an object is assigned with a call method to a function type, it adopts the features of an anonymous function.

© Sanjib Sinha 2020
S. Sinha, *Quick Start Guide to Dart Programming*,
https://doi.org/10.1007/978-1-4842-5562-9_8

179

Calling a class like a function is an interesting feature in Dart. All we need to do is just implement the `call()` method. Consider Figure 8-1, before we test some example code.

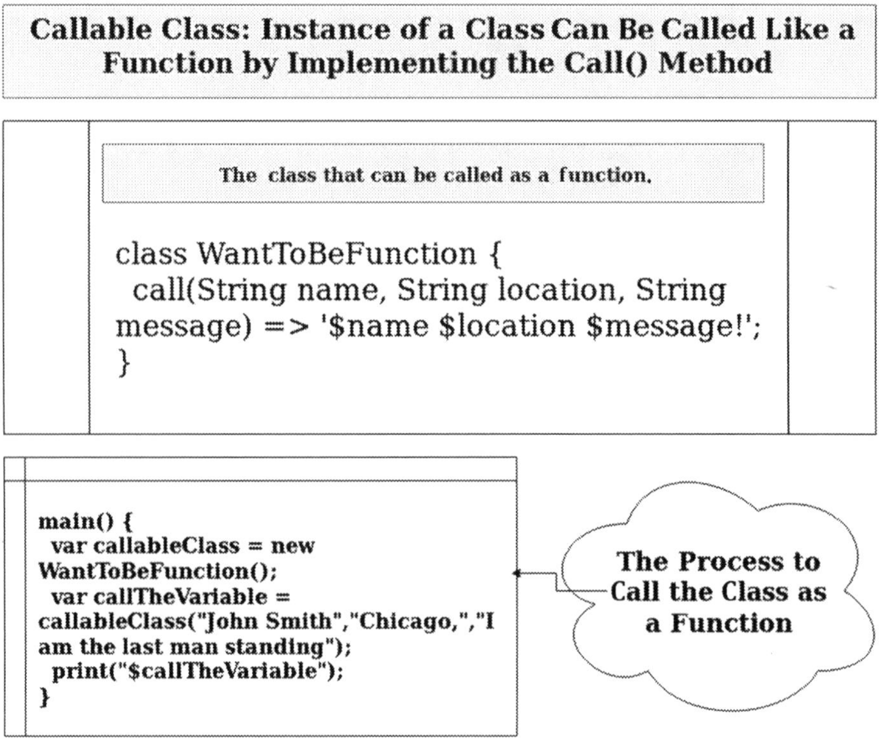

Callable Class: Instance of a Class Can Be Called Like a Function by Implementing the Call() Method

The class that can be called as a function.

```
class WantToBeFunction {
  call(String name, String location, String
  message) => '$name $location $message!';
}
```

```
main() {
  var callableClass = new
WantToBeFunction();
  var callTheVariable =
callableClass("John Smith","Chicago,","I
am the last man standing");
  print("$callTheVariable");
}
```

The Process to Call the Class as a Function

Figure 8-1. *Instance of a class implementing the call method*

Let's test some code and see the output.

```
//code 8.1
class CallableClassWithoutArgument {
  String output = "Callable class";
  void call() {
    print(output);
  }
}
```

```dart
class CallableClassWithArgument {
  call(String name) => "$name";
}

main(){
  var withoutArgument = CallableClassWithoutArgument();
  var withArgument = CallableClassWithArgument();
  withoutArgument(); // it is equivalent to withoutArgument.
                       call()
  print(withArgument("John Smith")); //OK.
  // withArgument(); //it'll give error
  print(withArgument.call("Calling John Smith"));
}
```

Here is the output of the preceding code:

```
//output of code 8.1
Callable class
John Smith
Calling John Smith
```

We can also use a callable class so that it can take an optional parameter. In the following code, the [name] parameter is optional in a callable class called Person:

```dart
//code 8.2
//when dart class is callable like a function, use call() function
class Person{
  String name;
  String call(String message, [name]){
    return "This message: '$message', has been passed to the
    person $name.";
  }
}
```

```
main(List<String> arguments){
  var John = Person();
  John.name = "John Smith";
  String name = John.name;
  String msgAndName = John("Hi John how are you?", name);
  print(msgAndName);
}
```

Here is the output:

```
This message: 'Hi John how are you?', has been passed to the
person John Smith.
```

Here, John is the variable, and Person() is the class. The class Person is called like a function because we have implemented the call() function, through which we have passed two parameters: String message and the optional parameter name. Finally, we have passed both and captured the value through msgAndName.

Future, Async, Await, and Asynchronous Programming

Because Dart is a single-threaded language, it is wrong to assume that we cannot use multithreaded, asynchronous programming in Dart. Before delving deep into asynchronous programming and how Dart manages to do it, you need to understand the basic mechanism of any Android application.

Whenever we switch on any Android device, the default process starts. It runs on the main UI thread. This main UI thread handles all core activities, such as button clicking, all types of touchscreen activities, etc. Still, these are not the only things we can expect from an Android device. We should be able to do some heavy operations such as checking mails, downloading files, watching movies, playing games, etc.

To do these heavy operations, Android allows parallel processing, which is multithreaded programming. It opens an application thread, and all the heavy operations are managed there.

When the heavy operations are going on in the background, we need our UI to be responsive; and for that reason, Android allows parallel processing.

This is the normal procedure of how asynchronous programming occurs.

Since Dart is a single-threaded programming language, it manages this asynchronous programming by using a feature called Future. In Dart SDK version 1.9, the Dart language has added asynchrony support. Now it is easier to write and read asynchronous Dart code. We will see that in a minute.

Let's first try to understand the whole concept, as shown in Figure 8-2.

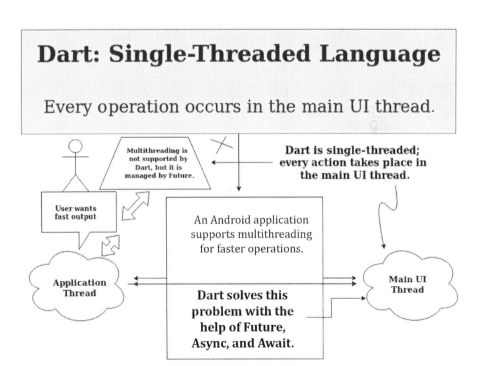

Figure 8-2. *How Dart manages asynchronous programming*

Before the features async and await were brought into Dart SDK version 1.9, Dart depended mainly on Future and then. We will look at some sample code to see how Dart Future manages the application thread parallel to the main UI thread. Consider the following code where we need to import the async libraries; we import predefined classes from the Dart libraries to add special features in our program:

```dart
//code 8.3
import 'dart:async';

// our all operations will use the main UI thread
//since dart and flutter are single threaded we need to use
  Future, Async amd Await APIs

void main(){
  // the main UI thread starts after that the heavy operations
    will take place
  print("The main UI thread is starting on here.");
  print("Now it will take 10 seconds to display news
  headlines.");
  displayNews();
  print("The main UI thread ends.");
  // this program remains incomplete, we don't get the result
  // it is because the main UI thread is overlapping before 10
    seconds
  // therefore we need await and async APIs to block main UI
    thread for 10 seconds
}

// this is where our heavy operations are taking place
Future<String> checkingNewsApp() {
  // since we are returning a string value
  // by delaying the main UI thread for 10 seconds
```

```
Future<String> delayingTenSeconds =  Future.
delayed(Duration(seconds: 10), (){
  return "The latest headlines are displayed here after
  10 seconds.";
});
// after 10 seconds the news headlines will be displayed
return delayingTenSeconds;
}

void displayNews() {
  // here we will primarily display the news headline
  Future<String> displayingNewsHeadlines = checkingNewsApp();
  // inside then we need an anonymous function like lambda or
    anonymous function
  displayingNewsHeadlines.then((displayString){
    // it will give the future object
    print("Displaying news headlines here:
    $displayingNewsHeadlines");
  });

}
```

In the output, we have gotten the value as a Future object.

```
//output of code 8.3
/home/ss/Downloads/flutter/bin/cache/dart-sdk/bin/dart
--enable-asserts --enable-vm-service:42565 /home/ss/
IdeaProjects/my_app/main.dart
Observatory listening on http://127.0.0.1:42565/vR6Xhf8qofo=/

The main UI thread is starting on here.
Now it will take 10 seconds to display news headlines.
The main UI thread ends.
Displaying news headlines here: Instance of 'Future<String>'

Process finished with exit code 0
```

If you read the comments in the program, you will understand how we got the Future object. However, our objective was different; we wanted to display news headlines instead of a Future object. A mistake was made in this line:

```
// it will give the future object
   print("Displaying news headlines here:
   $displayingNewsHeadlines");
 });
```

In the Future method, we passed an anonymous function where we have used a parameter. We need to check that line again. Let's write the code in this manner (changes appear in bold):

```
//code 8.4
import 'dart:async';

// our all operations will use the main UI thread
//since dart and flutter are single threaded we need to use
  Future, Async amd Await APIs

void main(){
  // the main UI thread starts after that the heavy operations
    will take place
  print("The main UI thread is starting on here.");
  print("Now it will take 10 seconds to display news headlines.");
  displayNews();
  print("The main UI thread ends.");
  // this program remains incomplete, we don't get the result
  // it is because the main UI thread is overlapping before
    10 seconds
  // therefore we need the Future API to block main UI thread
    for 10 seconds

}
```

```
// this is where our heavy operations are taking place
Future<String> checkingNewsApp() {
  // since we are returning a string value
  // by delaying the main UI thread for 10 seconds
  Future<String> delayingTenSeconds =  Future.
  delayed(Duration(seconds: 10), (){
    return "The latest headlines are displayed here after
    10 seconds.";
  });
  // after 10 seconds the news headlines will be displayed
  return delayingTenSeconds;
}

void displayNews() {
  // here we will primarily display the news headline
  Future<String> displayingNewsHeadlines = checkingNewsApp();
  // inside then we need an anonymous function like lambda or
    anonymous function
  displayingNewsHeadlines.then((displayString){
    print("Displaying news headlines here: $displayString");
  });

}
```

Now the output has been changed. Here is the news headlines we had initially wanted:

```
//output of code 8.4
/home/ss/Downloads/flutter/bin/cache/dart-sdk/bin/dart
--enable-asserts --enable-vm-service:42565 /home/ss/
IdeaProjects/my_app/main.dart
Observatory listening on http://127.0.0.1:42565/vR6Xhf8qofo=/
```

```
The main UI thread is starting on here.
Now it will take 10 seconds to display news headlines.
The main UI thread ends.
Displaying news headlines here: The latest headlines are
displayed here after 10 seconds.

Process finished with exit code 0
```

Now with the advent of the modern Dart versions, we have async and await. They help us write clean asynchronous code. Yet, you need to know how to use these features properly. They help us write asynchronous code that looks like synchronous code, while still using the Future API. In Dart 2, instead of suspending, it uses the await and async functions to execute synchronously.

Consider the following code where we have not used these features properly. Notice the long exception.

```
//code 8.5
import 'dart:async';

void main(){
  Future checkVersion() async {
    var version = await checkVersion();
    // Do something with version
    try {
      return version;
    } catch (e) {
      // React to inability to look up the version
      return e;
    }
  }
  print(checkVersion());
}
```

In the preceding code, we tried to print the version of the Dart SDK. We got this output:

```
//output of code 8.5
/home/ss/Downloads/flutter/bin/cache/dart-sdk/bin/dart
--enable-asserts --enable-vm-service:34325 /home/ss/
IdeaProjects/my_app/main.dart
Observatory listening on http://127.0.0.1:34325/pJXWzoNT9FO=/

Instance of 'Future<dynamic>'
Unhandled exception:
Stack Overflow
#0      _FutureListener.stateThenOnerror (dart:async/future_
        impl.dart:66:20)
#1      Future._thenNoZoneRegistration (dart:async/future_impl.
        dart:256:22)
#2      _awaitHelper (dart:async-patch/async_patch.dart:110:17)
#3      main.checkVersion (file:///home/ss/IdeaProjects/my_app/
        main.dart:5:19)
#4      _AsyncAwaitCompleter.start (dart:async-patch/async_
        patch.dart:49:6)
#5      main.checkVersion (file:///home/ss/IdeaProjects/my_app/
        main.dart:4:22)
#6      main.checkVersion (file:///home/ss/IdeaProjects/my_app/
        main.dart:5:37)
#7      _AsyncAwaitCompleter.start (dart:async-patch/async_
        patch.dart:49:6)
#8      main.checkVersion (file:///home/ss/IdeaProjects/my_app/
        main.dart:4:22)
#9      main.checkVersion (file:///home/ss/IdeaProjects/my_app/
        main.dart:5:37)
#10     _AsyncAwaitCompleter.start (dart:async-patch/async_
        patch.dart:49:6)
```

```
#11      main.checkVersion (file:///home/ss/IdeaProjects/my_app/
         main.dart:4:22)
#12      main.checkVersion (file:///home/ss/IdeaProjects/my_app/
         main.dart:5:37)
#13      _AsyncAwaitCompleter.start (dart:async-patch/async_
         patch.dart:49:6)
#14      main.checkVersion (file:///home/ss/IdeaProjects/my_app/
         main.dart:4:22)
#15      main.checkVersion (file:///home/ss/IdeaProjects/my_app/
         main.dart:5:37)
#16      _AsyncAwaitCompleter.start (dart:async-patch/async_
         patch.dart:49:6)
....
#11119   _AsyncAwaitCompleter.start (dart:async-patch/async_
         patch.dart:49:6)
#11120   main.checkVersion (file:///home/ss/IdeaProjects/my_app/
         main.dart:4:22)
#11121   main (file:///home/ss/IdeaProjects/my_app/main.
         dart:15:21)
#11122   _startIsolate.<anonymous closure> (dart:isolate-patch/
         isolate_patch.dart:301:19)
#11123   _RawReceivePortImpl._handleMessage (dart:isolate-patch/
         isolate_patch.dart:172:12)

Process finished with exit code 255
```

I have cut the output short for brevity. It was a long exception raised because of our mistake. If we had used the print statement, our problem would not have been solved. Then what will be the right form of writing async and await?

Consider the same code here:

```
//code 8.6
import 'dart:async';
void main(){

  print("The main UI thread is starting on here.");
  print("Now it will take 3 seconds to display the version of
  Dart.");
  checkVersion();
  print("The main UI thread ends.");
}

Future<String> checkingVersion() {
  // since we are returning a string value
  // by delaying the main UI thread for 3 seconds
  Future<String> delayingTenSeconds =  Future.
  delayed(Duration(seconds: 3), (){
    return "The version 2.1 is displayed here after 3 seconds.";
  });
  // after 3 seconds the version will be displayed
  return delayingTenSeconds;
}

void checkVersion() async {
  String version = await checkingVersion();
  // Do something with version
  try {
    print("Displaying version here: $version");
  } catch (e) {
    // React to inability to look up the version
    return e;
  }
}
```

In the preceding code, these lines are important:

```
Future<String> checkingVersion() {
  // since we are returning a string value
  // by delaying the main UI thread for 3 seconds
  Future<String> delayingTenSeconds =  Future.
  delayed(Duration(seconds: 3), (){
....
void checkVersion() async {
  String version = await checkingVersion();
```

What kind of Future method are we using? String. Therefore, the
async and await methods should follow that. Now our output is cleaner
than before, as shown here:

```
//output of code 8.6
/home/ss/Downloads/flutter/bin/cache/dart-sdk/bin/dart
--enable-asserts --enable-vm-service:41595 /home/ss/
IdeaProjects/my_app/main.dart
Observatory listening on http://127.0.0.1:41595/hMelJx-vdlw=/

The main UI thread is starting on here.
Now it will take 10 seconds to display news headlines.
The main UI thread ends.
Displaying version here: The version 2.1 is displayed here
after 3 seconds.

Process finished with exit code 0
```

Now we can use more async and await to understand how they
actually work with Future. We can head back to the news application. This
time, we will use async and await instead of Future then.

Consider the following code where we have not used async and await.
The main UI thread has finished, and after ten seconds we get the Future
object!

```
//code 8.7
import 'dart:async';

// our all operations will use the main UI thread
//since dart and flutter are single threaded we need to use
  Future, Async amd Await APIs
//however, we have not used it here and got the future object
  instead of headlines

void main(){
  // the main UI thread starts after that the heavy operations
    will take place
  print("The main UI thread is starting on here.");
  print("Now it will take 10 seconds to display news headlines.");
  displayNews();
  print("The main UI thread ends.");
  // this program remains incomplete, we don't get the result
  // it is because the main UI thread is overlapping before
    10 seconds
  // therefore we need await and async APIs to block main UI
    thread for 10 seconds

}


// this is where our heavy operations are taking place
Future<String> checkingNewsApp(){
  // since we are returning a string value
  // by delaying the main UI thread for 10 seconds
  Future<String> delayingTenSeconds =  Future.
  delayed(Duration(seconds: 10), (){
    return "The latest headlines are displayed here after
    10 seconds.";
  });
```

```
  // after 10 seconds the news headlines will be displayed
  return delayingTenSeconds;
}

void displayNews(){
  // here we will primarily display the news headline
  Future<String> displayingNewsHeadlines = checkingNewsApp();
  print("Displaying news headlines here:
  $displayingNewsHeadlines");
}
```

Our objective was to display the news headlines. Instead, we have gotten the Future object.

```
//output of code 8.7
/home/ss/Downloads/flutter/bin/cache/dart-sdk/bin/dart
--enable-asserts --enable-vm-service:35735 /home/ss/
IdeaProjects/my_app/main.dart
Observatory listening on http://127.0.0.1:35735/q812ySn2w1s=/

The main UI thread is starting on here.
Now it will take 10 seconds to display news headlines.
Displaying news headlines here: Instance of 'Future<String>'
The main UI thread ends.

Process finished with exit code 0
```

Now, we are going to use the async and await features properly to get the news headlines we wanted on the screen.

```
//code 8.8
import 'dart:async';

// our all operations will use the main UI thread
//since dart and flutter are single threaded we need to use
  Future, Async amd Await APIs
```

```
void main(){
  // the main UI thread starts after that the heavy operations
     will take place
  print("The main UI thread is starting on here.");
  print("Now it will take 10 seconds to display news
  headlines.");
  displayNews();
  print("The main UI thread ends.");
  // this program remains incomplete, we don't get the result
  // it is because the main UI thread is overlapping before
     10 seconds
  // therefore we need await and async APIs to block main UI
     thread for 10 seconds

}

// this is where our heavy operations are taking place
Future<String> checkingNewsApp() {
  // since we are returning a string value
  // by delaying the main UI thread for 10 seconds
  Future<String> delayingTenSeconds =  Future.
  delayed(Duration(seconds: 10), (){
    return "The latest headlines are displayed here after
    10 seconds.";
  });
  // after 10 seconds the news headlines will be displayed
  return delayingTenSeconds;
}
```

```
void displayNews() async {
  // here we will primarily display the news headline
  String displayingNewsHeadlines = await checkingNewsApp();
  print("Displaying news headlines here:
  $displayingNewsHeadlines");
}
```

This time we find the output has changed, and after the main UI thread has finished, it has displayed the news headlines after ten seconds.

```
//output of code 8.8
/home/ss/Downloads/flutter/bin/cache/dart-sdk/bin/dart
--enable-asserts --enable-vm-service:33305 /home/ss/
IdeaProjects/my_app/main.dart
Observatory listening on http://127.0.0.1:33305/FpBVOpOM2qc=/

The main UI thread is starting on here.
Now it will take 10 seconds to display news headlines.
The main UI thread ends.
Displaying news headlines here: The latest headlines are
displayed here after 10 seconds.

Process finished with exit code 0
```

In the next chapter, you will learn about Dart libraries and packages; furthermore, you need to know that Dart libraries have a lot of functions that return Future objects. These functions are all asynchronous. They handle time-consuming heavy operations (such as I/O). To do that, these functions use the async and await keywords; this lets us write the asynchronous code that looks like synchronous code.

Therefore, to handle Future properly and get the complete Future output, we need to use async and await; in addition, we can use the Future API's old methods like then(), catchError(), and whenComplete().

More on the Future API

Let's look at some more examples to understand how the Future API works. Consider the following code, where we use the Future delayed() method, and then using the then() method, we pass a lambda function to print the value.

```
//code 8.9
import 'dart:async';

void main(){
  Future<int>.delayed(
      Duration(seconds: 6),
      () { return 200; },
  ).then((value) { print(value); });
  print('Waiting for a value for 6 seconds...');
}
```

We have delayed the whole process for six seconds; then we return the value.

```
//output of code 8.9
/home/ss/Downloads/flutter/bin/cache/dart-sdk/bin/dart
--enable-asserts --enable-vm-service:35393 /home/ss/
IdeaProjects/my_app/main.dart
Observatory listening on http://127.0.0.1:35393/ushFPI8yST4=/

Waiting for a value for 6 seconds...
200

Process finished with exit code 0
```

As you see, according to the output of the value we are about to print, we need to mention what type of Future object we are going to use. In the preceding code, this line is important:

```
Future<int>.delayed()//
```

We need to declare the type of Future object. Here it is an integer because we are returning an integer.

In the next code snippet, instead of returning a concrete value, we are going to throw an exception:

```
//code 8.10
import 'dart:async';

void main(){
  Future<int>.delayed(
      Duration(seconds: 6),
      () => throw 'We are throwing some error here.',
  ).then((value) {
    print(value);
  });
  print('Waiting for a value');
}
```

Quite naturally, we get an error in the output.

```
//output of code 8.10
/home/ss/Downloads/flutter/bin/cache/dart-sdk/bin/dart
--enable-asserts --enable-vm-service:43091 /home/ss/
IdeaProjects/my_app/main.dart
Observatory listening on http://127.0.0.1:43091/8Zr4UnbBJMA=/

Waiting for a value_
Unhandled exception:
We are throwing some error here.
```

```
#0      main.<anonymous closure> (file:///home/ss/IdeaProjects/
        my_app/main.dart:6:13)
#1      new Future.delayed.<anonymous closure> (dart:async/
        future.dart:316:39)
#2      Timer._createTimer.<anonymous closure> (dart:async-
        patch/timer_patch.dart:21:15)
#3      _Timer._runTimers (dart:isolate-patch/timer_impl.
        dart:382:19)
#4      _Timer._handleMessage (dart:isolate-patch/timer_impl.
        dart:416:5)
#5      _RawReceivePortImpl._handleMessage (dart:isolate-patch/
        isolate_patch.dart:172:12)

Process finished with exit code 255
```

Finally, we would like to see how some old Future methods, such as catchError() and whenComplete(), work, as shown in the following code:

```
//code 8.11
import 'dart:async';

void main(){
  Future<int>.delayed(
      Duration(seconds: 6),
      () { return 100; },
  ).then((value) {
    print(value);
  }).catchError(
      (err) {
        print('Caught $err');
      },
```

```
    test: (err) => err.runtimeType == String,
  ).whenComplete(() { print("Process completed."); });
  print('The main UI thread is waiting');
}
```

As you can see, the main UI thread waits for six seconds and then produces the output.

```
//output of code 8.11
/home/ss/Downloads/flutter/bin/cache/dart-sdk/bin/dart
--enable-asserts --enable-vm-service:36707 /home/ss/
IdeaProjects/my_app/main.dart
Observatory listening on http://127.0.0.1:36707/AIbh2kXqMxM=/

The main UI thread is waiting
100
Process completed.

Process finished with exit code 0
```

Basically, the Future delays a thread for a few seconds, as mentioned earlier; then it produces either completed data or an error!

CHAPTER 9

Dart Packages and Libraries

Dart programming relies heavily on libraries, which contain critical sets of built-in functionality. Several common libraries are provided for you; in addition, you can do modular programming with the help of libraries. We have already seen many examples, such as predefined collection methods, many mathematical functions, etc.

Several common libraries serve many purposes for building Dart applications. So far, you have seen many built-in functions that we have used in our many user-defined functions. For example, the `dart:core` libraries provide assistance for numbers, string-specific operations, and collections. With the help of `dart:math`, we can do many types of mathematical operations quite easily.

We can also build our own libraries. In fact, as you progress, you will feel the necessity to create your own libraries. In addition, you can get additional libraries by importing them from packages.

Through packages, we can share software such as libraries and tools.

Basically, we can get help from both types of libraries (built-in and custom). Figure 9-1 shows you how we can use libraries and packages in Dart.

© Sanjib Sinha 2020
S. Sinha, *Quick Start Guide to Dart Programming*,
https://doi.org/10.1007/978-1-4842-5562-9_9

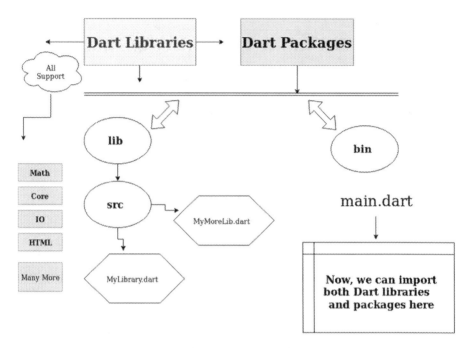

Figure 9-1. *Usages of Dart libraries and packages*

You should also know why we need libraries. To create a modular and shareable code base, the codebase needs to be well organized. In fact, this is an essential part of object-oriented programming. Libraries not only provide support for modular, object-oriented programming, but they also give you a kind of privacy in your own code.

Identifiers, starting with the underscore (_), are visible only in your libraries. A prepending underscore means this function is private to the library. That means you cannot use that function in other libraries. This is a typical Dart feature. Dart handles visibility with this prepending underscore.

Libraries also help you avoid name conflicts, which is an essential part of coding. Let's look at an example to clarify these points.

Importing Packages

First, let's create a RelationalOperators.dart file inside the lib folder.

```
//code 9.1
//lib/ RelationalOperators.dart
class TrueOrFalse{
  int firstNum = 40;
  int secondNum = 40;
  int thirdNum = 74;
  int fourthNum = 56;
  void BetweenTrueOrFalse(){
    if (firstNum == secondNum || thirdNum == fourthNum){
      print("If choice between 'true' or 'false', in this case
      the 'TRUE' gets the precedence. $firstNum is equal to
      $secondNum");
    } else print("Nothing happens.");
  }
  void BetweenTrueAndFalse(){
    if (firstNum == secondNum && thirdNum == fourthNum){
      print("It will go to else clause");
    } else print("If choice between 'true' and 'false', in
      this case the 'FALSE' gets the precedence. $thirdNum is
      not equal to $fourthNum");
  }
}
```

Next, create a file called PowProject.dart inside the lib folder.

```
//code 9.2
//lib/PowProject.dart
class PowProject{
  void MultiplyByAGivenNumber(int fixedNumber, int givenNumber){
```

```
    int result = fixedNumber * givenNumber;
    print(result);
  }
  void pow(int x, int y){
    int addition = x + y;
    print(addition);
  }
}
```

Now take a look at the main() function body, shown here:

```
//code 9.3
import 'dart:math' as math;
import 'package:IdeaProjects/PowProject.dart';
import 'package:IdeaProjects/RelationalOperators.dart' as
relation;

main(List<String> arguments){
  print("Printing 2 to the power 5 using Dart's built-in
  'dart:math' library.");
  var int = math.pow(2, 5);
  print(int);
  print("Now we are going to use another 'pow()' function from
  our own library.");
  var anotherPowObject = PowProject();
  anotherPowObject.MultiplyByAGivenNumber(4, 3);
  anotherPowObject.pow(2, 12);
  print("Now we are going to use another library to test the
  relational operators.");
  var trueOrFalse = relation.TrueOrFalse();
  trueOrFalse.BetweenTrueOrFalse();
  trueOrFalse.BetweenTrueAndFalse();
}
```

In the lib (or libraries) folder, we have created two classes. One of them has a function called pow(). But the built-in dart:math library has a function with the same name: pow(). We cannot use both of these same-name functions in the same code. It would give us errors. So, to avoid the name conflict, we have to create our own library and define it inside the class. Quite naturally, for the book's sake, our created pow() function is doing something different than calculating the power of a number.

Look at the top of the main() function, shown here:

```
import 'dart:math' as math;
import 'package:IdeaProjects/PowProject.dart';
import 'package:IdeaProjects/RelationalOperators.dart' as
Relation;
```

We have used the keyword import to specify how our libraries, besides the core libraries, can be used. Our project directory is IdeaProjects, and PowProject.dart is inside the lib directory. The path after the project directory comes from inside the lib directory. After import, we need to pass an argument, which is nothing but a uniform resource identifier (URI) specifying the libraries. For any built-in libraries, the URI has the special dart:... scheme. For other libraries, you can use the file system path or the package:... scheme.

When we directly use the libraries, we use a normal line like this:

```
import 'package:IdeaProjects/PowProject.dart';
```

In that case, we can directly create the class object that belongs to that particular library, as follows:

```
var anotherPowObject = PowProject();
```

However, there is another good method; we can call any library by using a name, like this:

```
import 'package:IdeaProjects/RelationalOperators.dart' as
relation;
```

The advantage to this is that now we can create any class object belonging to that library using the new name, as follows:

```
var trueOrFalse = relation.TrueOrFalse();
```

These prefixes are used to avoid name conflicts and to simplify long package names. You can write same-name classes in libraries, and you can use them by giving them a name.

Using Built-in Dart Libraries

A few good built-in libraries come with Dart; you do not need to write them again. Here are some of them:

- `dart:core`: This gives us many core functionalities. It is automatically imported into every Dart program.

- `dart:math`: You have seen how we have used the core mathematical library in our program. We can do many types of mathematical operations using this library, such as generate random numbers.

- `dart:convert`: Converting between different data representations is made easy through this library; this conversion includes JSON and UTF-8.

Writing a Server Using Dart

By using the default Dart libraries, we can easily build a local server, request an HTML page, and get the response. In the first half of this section, we will see how to include an HTML file in our program and get a response in the client browser. For the server-client relationship, which is the foundation of any kind of web application, our Dart program will play the role of the server, and the client will be the browser that we will use.

Showing Some Simple Text

Let's write some simple Dart back-end server code that will output a string response.

```dart
//code 9.4
import 'dart:io';
import 'dart:async';

Future main() async {
  var myServer = await HttpServer.bind(
    '127.0.0.1',
    8080,
  );
  print("The server is alive on the above mentioned port and
  it's listening "
      "on ${myServer.port}/");

  myServer.listen((HttpRequest myRequest){
    myRequest.response
      ..write("Bonjour mademoiselle, comment appelez vous?")
      ..close();
  });
}
```

The main() function starts with Future and async, and later we use await. We discussed these concepts in the previous chapter. Then, we use the HttpServer.bind() method to create an HttpServer object. In the bind() method, we pass two parameters: the host (127.0.0.1) and the port (8080). Here, we use a simple print statement to give some simple output to show we are listening to the previously mentioned port.

Now, according to the server-client relationship structure, our new server object should listen for a new HttpRequest object (here myRequest). And, after receiving a request, the server object should respond. The response object calls a write() method that gives us some simple output like this:

```
"Bonjour mademoiselle, comment appelez vous?"
```

This is a French sentence that means, "Good day, Miss, what are you called?"

Now, after running this program, we should type http://127.0.0.1:8080 in any browser. It will give this output. We can run this program using two methods. You can just run it on Android Studio or IntelliJ Community, and in the console you will get the message that the server is listening. After that, we can open the browser to see the output. In another method, we can use our terminal. Open the project folder's bin directory and type the following:

```
//code 9.5
dart main.dart
```

This will also run the program (Figure 9-2).

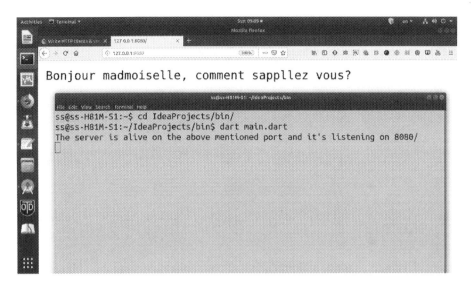

Figure 9-2. *Dart back-end server-client program*

Here is a caveat. You should not run two programs listening to the same port in parallel to each other. If the port is already in use, the connection will automatically be refused. You can use any port number from 1024 and higher.

If you run the same program on Android Studio, you will get the "server listening" message in the console (Figure 9-3).

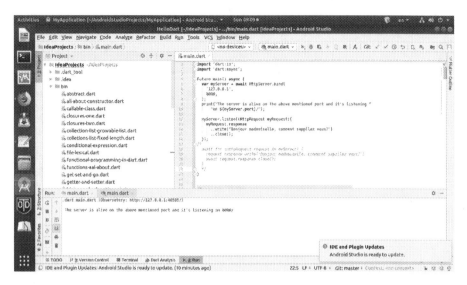

Figure 9-3. *Running the same program through Android Studio*

To stop the program in the terminal, you can press Control+C, and in any IDE console, you click the red button on the left side. You will see it in the top-right corner also.

Once the program is stopped, it gives us output like this:

```
//code 9.6
```

```
/home/ss/flutter/bin/cache/dart-sdk/bin/dart --enable-vm-
service:40505 /home/ss/IdeaProjects/bin/main.dart
Observatory listening on http://127.0.0.1:40505/
```

The server is alive on the above mentioned port and it's listening on 8080/

Process finished with exit code 137 (interrupted by signal 9: SIGKILL)

Up to now, we were able to give a simple response as output through our back-end server-client program. Furthermore, we can make our back-end server display an HTML page.

Showing an HTML Page

The process is not very complicated. All we need is an HTML file first. Let's create a simple HTML5 file called index.html in our root directory.

```
//code 9.7

<!doctype html>

<html lang="en">
<head>
    <meta charset="utf-8">

    <title>A Dart WEB Example on Local Server</title>
    <meta name="description" content="The HTML5 Herald">
    <meta name="author" content="SitePoint">

</head>

<body>
<h1>A Dart WEB Example on Local Server</h1>
<a href="https://sanjibsinha.fun" about="It's my unofficial
site" onclick="Click Me!">
    Here is my unofficial site!
</a>
</body>
</html>
```

Let's see the file in Android Studio first (Figure 9-4).

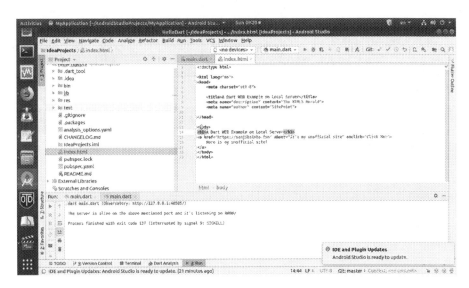

Figure 9-4. *The index.html file in the Android Studio root directory*

Now we can call this index.html file to get its contents in the browser. As you saw earlier, the Dart libraries have all the tools to build any kind of web application. Here we need to use our response object to return the contents of our HTML file, setting its Content-Type header to HTML:

```
//code 9.8
import 'dart:io';
import 'dart:async';

final File myFile = File("index.html");

Future main() async {
  var myServer = await HttpServer.bind(
    '127.0.0.1',
    8080,
  );
```

```
print("The server is alive on the above mentioned port and
it's listening "
    "on ${myServer.port}/");
// we are going to use the await from dart async library
await for (HttpRequest myRequest in myServer) {

  if(await myFile.exists()){
    print("We're going to serve ${myFile.path}");
    myRequest.response.headers.contentType = ContentType.html;

    await myFile.openRead().pipe(myRequest.response);

  }

}

}
```

After reading the file, we have used the pipe() method to put the contents of the file into the response, which will give us the response (Figure 9-5).

Figure 9-5. *The response of an HTML file using the Dart back-end server technique*

Now, we can even check the source to see that the HTML file was used for this purpose (Figure 9-6).

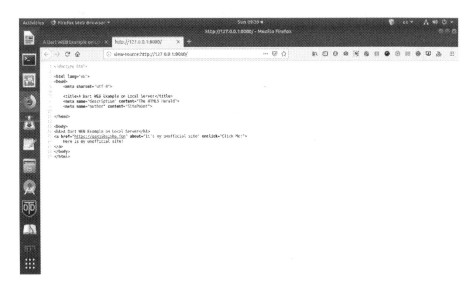

Figure 9-6. *The view source of the HTML file displayed in the browser*

You have seen how we can use Dart libraries for many types of complicated application development. We can also easily build our own packages using these libraries to reuse this code in other applications.

What's Next

There's no doubt that Dart will be even more popular in the future. Not only is it popular in the iOS and Android worlds, but it is being used in web applications. This book served as a short introduction to Dart. Good luck in the future.

Index

A, B

Abstract classes
definition, 117
key points, 118
object-oriented programming
languages, 119–121
source code, 118
Anonymous function
closure, 146–149
definition, 141
higher-order functions, 145
lambdas
key features of, 145
longhand version, 142, 143
parameters, 143
shorthand code, 144
type of, 142
variable, 142
types of, 149–152
Asynchronous programming, 182

C

Callable classes, 179
call() method, 179, 180
Person() method, 181
source code, 180, 181
Closure, 146–149

Collections
data structures (*see* Data
structures and collections)
lists (ordered group), 155
default methods, 159, 160
map() function, 161, 162
source code, 156, 157
types of, 155
maps, 166–171
queue, 176–177
set (unordered collections),
162–166
unique items, 162
validations (lists and maps),
171–175
Constructors, 81–84
default and a named
constructor, 100–102

D

Dart language, 1
arrays, 27, 28
assignment operators, 39, 40
built-in types, 17–19
code editors, 2
features, 2, 4
get, set, go, 29–33

Dart language (*cont.*)
    IDE, 4
    importing packages, 203–206
    List objects, 27
    lookup() method, 29
    number and double types, 19–21
    operators, 33–35
    overview, 2
    relational/equality
        operators, 35–39
    string interpolation, 18
    strings, 22–27
    boolean literals (true and
        false), 26
    type test operators, 38, 39
    value of variables, 18, 19
    variables store references, 14–16
Data structures and collections
    concepts of, 153
    type of, 153, 154

E

Entity relationships
    characteristics, 116
    composition relationship, 117
    derive features, 115
    differences, 114
    instantiation relationship, 117
    mammal entities, 116
    utilization relationship, 117
Exception handling
    built-in classes, 133, 134
    catch block, 135

    errors, 132, 134
    finally block, 136
    inputValue() function, 139
    single codebase, 137–139
    stack trace, 136
    syntax of, 135
    types of, 137

F, G

Flow control and looping, 43
    AND condition, 46
    conditional expressions, 49
    continue keyword, 62, 63
    if-else, 43–49
    for labels, 60–63
    for loop, 50–53
    looping code, 56–59
    OR condition, 47
    switch and case keywords, 63–65
    while and do-while, 53–56
Function DividingByFour(), 146
Functions
    fat arrow, 71
    lexical scope, 87–89
    main() function, 68–70
    parameter, 91–93
    points, 67
    recursive function, 72, 73
Future classes
    API, 197–200
    async and await, 184–186, 194
    asynchronous programming, 183
    Future delayed() method, 197

long exception, 188–190
    method, 192
    object, 186–188
    print statement, 190
    then() method, 197
    UI thread, 192, 196

H

Higher-order functions, 145

I, J

Inheritance
    default and a named
        constructor, 100–102
    main() function, 103
    multilevel inheritance (*see*
        Multilevel inheritance)
    single inheritance
        Animal class, 98, 99
        subclasses and
            superclasses, 99
    subclass, 97
    superclass, 97
insiderFunction(), 88
Integrated development
    environment (IDE), 4
    Android Studio, 9–11
    commands, 6
    IntelliJ IDEA community edition
        button installation, 7–9
        console, 9
        Dart plugins, 8

source code, 11–13
    version of, 5
Integrated development
    environments (IDEs), 3
Interfaces
    abstract class, 126, 127
    advantage of, 130
    Customers() method, 128–130
    definition, 121
    output results, 125
    source code, 121, 122
    standard structure, 123, 124
isTurnedOn() method, 73, 75

K

Key-value pairs, 166–171

L

Lambdas, 142
LetUsDivide() function, 146
Libraries and
    packages, 201
    built-in, 206
    import packages, 203–206
    server, 206
        Android Studio, 210
        back-end server-client
            program, 209
        back-end server
            technique, 213
        HTML page, 211–214
        index.html file, 212

Libraries and packages (*cont.*)
    simple text, 207–210
    view source data, 214
  use of, 201, 202

M, N

Mixins, 108–111
Multilevel inheritance, 97, 104–108

O, P, Q, R

Object-Oriented Programming
    (OOP)
  constructors, 81–84, 93–95
  digging deep, 77
  getter and setter, 89

hourOfSleep and
    numberOfFish, 79
implement classes, 84–87
lexical scope, 87–89
loosely coupled, 85
parameters, 90–92
properties and
    methods, 77
source code, 78
Objects, 73–76

S, T, U, V, W, X, Y, Z

Single inheritance, 97
Static variables and
    methods, 130–132
String interpolation, 18, 23

Printed in the United States
By Bookmasters